THE CRAFT BEER KITCHEN

A FRESH AND CREATIVE APPROACH TO COOKING WITH BEER

By Cooper Brunk
Photography & Styling by Christopher Cina
Foreword by Kim Jordan (Cofounder and CEO of New Belgium Brewing)

Craft Beer&Brewing

Edited by Jamie Bogner and Trish Faubion
Recipe testing by Christopher Cina and Stephanie Cina
Art direction and design by Jamie Bogner
Photography by Christopher Cina

Unfiltered Media Group, LLC
214 S. College Ave., Ste. 3
Fort Collins, CO 80524
beerandbrewing.com

ISBN: 978-0-9962689-0-5

Library of Congress Control Number: 2015938683

Printed in China through Asia Pacific Offset

10 9 8 7 6 5 4 3 2 1

CONTENTS

FOREWORD

Good beer has always been my drink of choice. When we started New Belgium Brewing in the basement of our home, we knew right away that our earliest beers, steeped in Belgian tradition, would pair wonderfully with a wide array of cuisines. There are of course classic examples of this—such as moules frites (mussels and fries) and a good Belgian wit beer—but what about Fat Tire and a grilled lamb chop or Trippel paired with wasabi-dusted scallops? The possibilities are endless, and the joy is in the exploration and discovery.

Beer pairs wonderfully and in its own way with food, just as many feel that wine does. For me, it's really about where I am and the company I'm with—such as that special moment when I'm with great friends and someone pulls out a bottle of Oude Kriek they've collected on a visit to Oud Beersel. By pairing it with the proper dish, we have the opportunity to experience that beer for the first time all over again and to remember why we fell in love with it in the first place.

Beer can evoke travel—all the places you've been to and remember fondly. The Orval in your glass started life far away in a beautiful monastery where you've walked the grounds. You can still see the afternoon light filtering through the leaves. You are transported in both time and place—and at the same time, you are experiencing that beer anew.

In these pages you will find many wonderful beer and food pairings that will inspire and transport you. My advice is to experiment, play around, have fun. Are you trying to pair for contrast—a spicy shrimp Creole with a bright, hoppy IPA—or do you want flavors that complement such as a Belgian dubbel and a wedge of chocolate torte?

Consider the time of year and see what ingredients you can source fresh and locally. Think about the people you're cooking for and what might surprise and delight their senses.

In the end, you get to create these shared moments that will become fond memories, and the beer in your glass will evoke the light and the laughter of good times had and still to come. That's the power and beauty of pairing a fine and transcendent beer with creative, inspired dishes you prepared in your kitchen.

Salud!

Kim Jordan
CEO and Cofounder, New Belgium Brewing

INTRODUCTION

When it comes to fine cuisine, chefs around the world are finally waking up to the fact that beer is just as good—if not better —for cooking with than wine. The breadth of beers styles gives chefs a wealth of options—whether it's a smoky porter, a crisp pilsner, or a bitter IPA, the beer you cook with can add flavors to your cooking like no wine can. But recipes for cooking with beer (beyond the routine pub fare) have been few and far between. The world doesn't need another recipe for beer-can chicken, bratwurst braised in beer, or beer-battered onion rings.

Craft brewers around the world are increasingly taking cues from the culinary world and are pushing boundaries with their beer—adding fruit, spicing beer with flavors such as mole, or conditioning pilsners on shaved black truffles—but the culinary world has been slower to embrace craft beer as an ingredient and a pairing partner for fine cuisine. The goal of this book is to help accelerate that acceptance and show that beer can be flavorful, nuanced, and sophisticated both as part of a fine dish and when paired with one.

Throughout the book, I've offered suggestions for beers to cook with, but please take these as just a starting point for your own cooking. As with food, taste in beer is very personal, and you should use beer with flavors your prefer. The best ingredients to cook with are fresh and local, and a number of beer styles (such as IPA or pale ale) are also best when consumed as fresh as possible, so get out to your local farmer's market for fresh produce, then swing by your local well-respected craft brewery and pick up some great beer.

Whether you're cooking for family, friends, or yourself, you owe it to yourself to explore the flavors that beer can add to your dishes. Dive into these recipes—some brand-new, some old favorites—for a taste of what beer can offer.

Hoppy Cooking!

Cooper Brunk

Legend

Throughout the book, we use these symbols:

 TIME

 INGREDIENTS

 BEER RECOMMENDATION

GUIDE TO BEER GLASSWARE

We all taste first with our eyes before we take a bite or a sip, and that visual component is just as important when serving beer as it is when preparing food. Appropriate and stylish beer glassware that beautifully presents beer can place your guests in a more receptive state of mind for the flavors in the food and beer that you're sharing with them. In addition, different glasses play to the strengths of different styles of beer, whether it's helping to focus aromas, produce a more attractive head for the beer, release the volatile aromatics, or simply showcase the beautiful color of the beer. Here, we've identified and demystified some of the major glassware styles so you can put the right beer in the right glass with the right dish every time. The best meals are made from a combination of great food, fantastic company, and compelling presentation, and while the right glassware won't make or break a meal, it will certainly add to the experience.

DIMPLED MUG
Sturdy and social, the dimpled mug is a staple for English pub and German beer–hall-style beers (think amber German lagers such as Marzen and Oktoberfest and British-ale styles such as ESB, mild, pale ale, or dry stout.

ENGLISH NONIC PINT
The go-to glass for British-beer styles that range from pale ales and IPAs to milds and bitters, the nonic pint is also great for lower ABV sessionable stouts and porters. One defining feature (and advantage over the more common Shaker pint) are the thinner walls—they won't change the temperature of your beer as rapidly as the thicker Shaker-pint walls.

PILSNER
Visually stunning, the pilsner glass shows off crisp beers in their best light. The tall and thin body generates a tall and attractive head for your beer. It's perfect for pilsners and light American lagers, but can also be used for darker German-lager styles such as Schwarzbier.

WEIZEN GLASS
Built for wheat beers, the weizen glass features a bowled top to create more space for that signature luscious head (the additional protein content in wheat beers aids in head creation and retention). That head isn't just a visual cue, however—it delivers the yeast-derived aromatics that the beers are known for. Use with American wheat styles as well as hefeweizen, weizenbock, and dunkleweizen.

SNIFTER

The deep bowl of the snifter glass focuses and delivers the rich aromas of strong beer styles such as barleywine, imperial stout, and any bigger beer that has spent time in a barrel (Scotch ale, old ale, etc.). Swirl gently, then stick your nose in the glass and breathe deeply to get the full aroma experience—much of what we perceive as "taste" is actually smell, and the snifter is built to maximize it.

TULIP

Traditionally associated with Belgian styles such as saison, the tulip glass has now evolved into the defacto standard craft-beer glass at many breweries and craft-beer bars. The shape is great for aromatic beers such as imperial IPAs, and their similarity to snifters makes them great for barleywines and big stouts. If you buy only one specialty beer glass, make it a footed tulip. Its versatility is unmatched in the beer-glass world.

CHALICE (OR GOBLET)

Glassware can be as much about marketing as it is about presentation, and many Belgian beers have custom-branded versions of the chalice. But it's the right choice for serving Belgian (and Belgian-style) dubbel, tripel, and quadrupel as well as Belgian dark strong ale and even Berliner weisse.

WHITE WINE GLASS

For entertaining at home, it's convenient to use one set of glasses for multiple purposes, and serving beer in wine glasses can definitely be a conversation starter. White wine glasses are the right size for smaller pours of bigger beers that would otherwise look out-of-scale in larger glasses (red wine glasses tend to be too large). Wine glasses are suitable for big beer styles (imperial stout, barleywine, etc.) but also lambic, gueuze, and wild ale.

FLUTE

Highly carbonated, bright, and colorful beer such as lambic is showcased beautifully in a flute glass. The narrow shape creates an impressive champagne-like head and allows the glass to showcase the beer's color.

SPECIALTY GLASSES

Glassmakers have jumped on the growing craft-beer market in recent years with increasing numbers of specialty glasses. Rastal's Teku (left) is a stylized tulip glass aimed at high-end beer styles such as imperial stout, barleywine, and wild ale, while Spiegelau's IPA glass (right) is purpose-designed for releasing and concentrating intense hops aromatics. The thin glass walls of both are highly refined and present beer very well.

PAIRING CRAFT BEER AND FOOD

When it comes to pairing with food, beer has an in-built advantage over wine. While wine has three ingredients to work with and a (relatively) limited range of flavors, the stylistic range of beer is vast. Beer can taste like bananas or cloves (if the brewer uses Belgian yeast strains), citrus fruit (with the right hops varieties or *Brettanomyces* yeast), dark roasted coffee, aged bourbon ... the list goes on.

In addition, the flavorful ingredient additions to beer—everything from cocoa nibs to tea leaves to hot chiles—are only constrained by the brewer's good taste and vision. The result is beer's chameleon-like ability to pair with any dish at any meal from brunch to dessert. The challenge, however, is to navigate the myriad options and settle on a strategy for your own pairing. Here are a couple of ways to think about food and beer pairings that can inform your own decision making.

Contrast

Opposites attract. This is the riskier approach to pairing, but when it works, it can really pay off. Pair a sour beer with a sweet dish or a malty stout with briny seafood or a pungent blue cheese. Contrasting pairings can work best when the dish you are pairing has a singular dominant flavor or texture characteristic. The contrasting beer can bring balance to the dish by toning down the dominant characteristic of the food but leaving intact the flavor that made you choose the dish in the first place. For example, a dish with a heavy alfredo cream sauce can be tempered with the bitterness and cutting power of a highly carbonated fresh pale ale. Pairing a crisp, clean IPA with an oily fish can add a new dimension to both the fish and the beer (not to mention the fat of the fish heightens your tastebuds' perception of the beer's bitterness). Pairing that same IPA with a complex dish such as Mole Poblano can keep the over-the-top richness of the mole from becoming overpowering.

Complement

If you are looking for complementing flavors, you're looking for perfect-pitch harmony between the two. Think about the aroma, flavor, and mouthfeel of the dish. Which beers help accentuate those elements, raising them to an even higher level? For example, if you are making a dish that has deep roasted aromas and flavors, consider what kinds of beer have the same types of roast characteristics. Slow-roasted ribs pair well with a nice barleywine. The smoked flavor of the ribs meshes beautifully with the roasted character of the barleywine's malt, while the sweet and tangy spiciness of the barbecue sauce matches the residual sweetness in the beer, and the strength of flavors in both means that one does not outweigh the other.

For lighter, more delicate fare, a general rule of thumb is to serve lighter, more delicate beers. You can create excellent beer pairings with everything from salad to sorbet. Match the intensity of the beer to the intensity of your dish.

Carbonation

Most craft beer on the market is carbonated with carbon dioxide. Carbonation occurs naturally in bottle-conditioned beers as the yeast creates carbon dioxide as a by-product of the fermentation process. Some beers, however, are carbonated with nitrogen (nitro), which has a smaller carbonation bubble than carbon dioxide and results in a smooth, creamier mouthfeel. Depending on the effect you want, these can be a great way to smooth out really salty or greasy foods—one of the reasons that Guinness (on nitro, and cask before that) has been a favorite of fish and chips lovers for hundreds of years.

Serving

One of the mistakes many cooks make is thinking that they have to pair a single dish with an entire beer. Nothing could be further from the truth. You want to serve just enough to get the most flavor out of the dish, while leaving the palate refreshed. Think one sip for each bite of food. One rule of thumb is to serve a half ounce of beer for every bite on the plate. Your guests won't be drinking after every bite, but you want to make sure that they can start and finish with a mouthful of beer. You might serve only 4 ounces of beer with a light appetizer, while the entrée may require a full pint.

Remember, too, that beer should rarely be just sipped. Make sure your guests know to inhale, take a mouthful of beer, and exhale through the nose to get the maximum flavor, aroma, and experience.

Temperature

Don't forget serving temperature. Many beers actually taste better when they've had a chance to warm up a little bit. While not a hard and fast rule, the higher the alcohol content of the beer, the warmer it should be served. There are plenty of exceptions to this (some farmhouse ales, Goses, etc.), but make sure you are serving your beer at the correct temperature and planning accordingly.

Suggested serving temperatures:

🌡 BELOW 39°F (4°C)

Most refrigerators chill to between 36 and 38°F (2 and 3°C), so consider this "straight from the refrigerator" temperature. Beers served at this temperature will be difficult to taste, so this temperature is best for American light lagers and other large-scale commercial brews.

🌡 40°–44°F (4–7°C)

After taking a beer out of the refrigerator, let it sit for five minutes and (depending on the ambient air temperature) it should achieve this perfect serving temperature for Berliner weisse, Belgian (and Belgian-style) wit, German and Czech pilsner, weizen and wheat styles, kölsch, dark lager, and similar styles.

🌡 45°–54° (7–12°C)

Ten to fifteen minutes out of the fridge, and your beer should hit this temperature range, which is ideal for ale styles such as Belgian golden ale, tripel, saison, porter, dry stout, American pale ale, American IPA, imperial IPA, and amber ale plus lager styles such as dunkel, Vienna lager, Altbier, Helles, Schwarzbier, and similar styles.

🌡 55°–57° (13–14°C)

A few minutes longer, and your beer will reach "cellar temp," which is great for English-style ales such as ESB, brown ale, English pale ale, and old ale. This temperature is also great for Belgian ales such as lambic, gueuze, Flanders red and oud bruin, bière de garde, saison, abbey dubbel, and Belgian strong ale, as well as Scottish ale, Baltic porter, and similar styles.

🌡 58°–MID 60° (14–18°C)

High ABV beers need warmer serving temperatures to express their full range of flavors, so beer styles such as barleywine, imperial stout, dopplebock, and abbey quadrupel are best served here. This temperature is also suitable for cask ales served on traditional hand pumps.

Know Your Guests

Individuals have personal preferences that can override or add nuance to potential pairings. Make sure you take those beer preferences into account as you develop your menu. You wouldn't serve a steak to someone who hates red meat, so don't serve an imperial stout to someone who you know doesn't like big, dark ales.

While there are many different factors that go into making a great pairing, there are arguably only two primary approaches that cooks must consider with each dish they are trying to pair. Ask yourself this: Do I want a beer that is going to contrast with the flavors in this dish or complement them? Both approaches can create incredible results.

Use the cooking and pairing suggestions throughout this book as a starting point, and as you taste the beers in (and with) these dishes, try articulating why these particular suggestions and pairings work within the context of the dish, then go forth and experiment on your own.

PAIRING CRAFT BEER AND CHEESE

While wine will never go out of style as a partner to cheese, beer is definitely coming into its own. When you're creating your own pairings, consider first the intensity of the beer and cheese flavors, then your strategy (complement or contrast), then take a look at some of our suggested (and tested) pairings to the right for some interesting and unexpected combinations. A cheese and beer course with creative combinations can be the perfect way to set the tone for a larger meal, but there's never a bad time to pull a dry and spicy blue from the fridge and pair with a roasty imperial stout!

IPA & IMPERIAL IPA	CHEDDAR, SPICY CHEESE, AND EVEN BLUE CHEESE	Match the sharpness of the cheddar to the hoppiness of your IPA.
BELGIAN DUBBEL & TRIPEL	EMMETALER, GRUYÈRE, AND SIMILAR	Belgian beers are known for the flavors their yeast esters produce. Pair with similar cheeses to complement.
WIT & WHEAT	FRESH CHÈVRES, MOZZARELLA	Pair the subtle lighter flavors of fresh cheeses with similar light beer.
PILSNER & KÖLSCH	FRESH CHÈVRES, MOZZARELLA	Pair the subtle lighter flavors of fresh cheeses with similar light beer.
SWEET STOUT	BLUE CHEESE (SWEET & CREAMY)	Choose a blue with more caramel and toffee character; pair with oatmeal or chocolate stout or vanilla porter.
IMPERIAL STOUT	BLUE CHEESE (DRY & SPICY)	The sharper cheese flavor is a better foil for the roastier notes in the beer.
SAISON, BIÈRE DE GARDE & FARMHOUSE ALE	BRIE OR CAMEMBERT	The earthiness of the beer pairs well with the earthy cheese.
BARLEYWINE & BELGIAN QUAD	WASHED-RIND CHEESE	Washing the rind lets bacteria thrive, creating stronger and more defined flavors. Pair with an equally strong beer.
BOCK & DUNKEL	ALPINE-STYLE SEMIHARD CHEESE	The nutty and caramel flavors in the beer complement similar flavors in Comté and other alpine-style cheese.

Note: These pairing suggestions are a starting point and are by no means exhaustive. Use them to inspire your own pairings and develop pairings that work for your personal taste.

BREAKFAST
AND
BRUNCH

ACTIVE PREP: 10 minutes
TOTAL TIME: 60 minutes
MAKES: 1 loaf

10 Tbs (1 stick + 2 Tbs) unsalted butter, divided

1¾ cup all-purpose flour plus 2 Tbs for dusting the pan

¾ cup sugar

2 overripe bananas

2 eggs

1 Tbs (½ fl oz/15 ml) vanilla

½ cup (4 fl oz/118 ml) weizenbock

1 Tbs baking powder

Pinch of kosher salt

1 cup nuts, coarsely chopped (optional)

Sierra Nevada Weizenbock
(CHICO, CA)

Victory Brewing Moonglow Weizenbock
(DOWNINGTOWN, PA)

Southern Tier Goat Boy
(LAKEWOOD, NY)

Neshaminy Creek Neshaminator
(CROYDON, PA)

Weizenbock Banana Bread

Preheat the oven to 350°F (177°C). Coat the inside of a loaf pan with 2 tablespoons of butter. Dust with the 2 tablespoons of flour. Tap out any excess flour.

In a stand mixer fitted with a paddle attachment, cream the remaining 8 tablespoons of butter and the sugar at medium speed for 2–3 minutes until light and fluffy. Add the bananas and beat for an additional minute. Add the eggs one at a time while the mixer is running. Add the vanilla and beer. Reduce the speed to low. In a separate bowl, combine the dry ingredients except the nuts and add in three separate stages to the liquid mixture. Stop the mixer and scrape down the sides of the mixing bowl with a spatula. Fold in the nuts. Pour the batter into the buttered loaf pan. Bake for 55–60 minutes or until a toothpick inserted in the bread comes out clean. Transfer to a wire rack and cool for 10–15 minutes. Remove from the pan and cool completely before slicing.

ACTIVE PREP: 25 minutes
TOTAL TIME: 2–3½ hours
SERVES: 4

Beer-Bread French Toast with Maple Nut Brown Ale Syrup

Beer Bread

3 cup all-purpose flour
1 cup (8 fl oz/237 ml) beer
1 package instant yeast
4 Tbs (½ stick) unsalted butter, melted
2 egg yolks
1 Tbs kosher salt
Pinch of sugar

French Toast

4 eggs
2 cup (16 fl oz/473 ml) heavy cream
1 cup sugar
2 Tbs (1 fl oz/30 ml) vanilla extract
1 Tbs cinnamon
1 tsp nutmeg
1 Tbs orange zest
Splash of maple nut brown ale
1 loaf of beer bread sliced into 1" slices
4 Tbs (½ stick) unsalted butter

Syrup

1 cup (8 fl oz/237 ml) maple nut brown ale
½ cup (4 fl oz/118 ml) pure maple syrup
½ cup brown sugar
1 Tbs cornstarch

Tommyknocker Maple Nut Brown Ale
(IDAHO SPRINGS, CO)
Dogfish Head Immort Ale
(MILTON, DE)

BEER BREAD

Preheat the oven to 400°F (204°C). Combine all the ingredients in the bowl of a stand mixer with a dough-hook attachment. Mix on medium speed for 3–5 minutes. Reduce speed to low and continue to knead for 10–12 minutes. Place the dough in a large bowl and cover tightly with plastic wrap. Let the dough rise for 1–2 hours or until doubled in volume. Punch down and shape into a loaf. Place in a buttered loaf pan and cover with plastic wrap. Let the dough rise a second time for 30 minutes to an hour. Remove the plastic wrap. Bake in the preheated oven for 20–25 minutes. Remove from the oven and let cool completely before slicing.

FRENCH TOAST

Preheat a griddle or large sauté pan over medium heat. In a large bowl, combine the eggs, cream, sugar, vanilla extract, cinnamon, nutmeg, orange zest, and beer. Whisk well to combine thoroughly. Dip each slice of bread in the custard mixture being sure to coat each side. Melt the butter in the sauté pan and coat well. Place coated bread slices onto the griddle and cook for 3–5 minutes per side.

SYRUP

In a small saucepan, combine all the ingredients. Whisk thoroughly while bringing to a boil over medium-high heat. Remove the pan from the heat. Let cool slightly before serving over French toast.

ACTIVE PREP: 15 minutes
TOTAL TIME: 25 minutes
SERVES: 2

Beer Mornay Sauce

1 cup (8 fl oz/237 ml) whole milk
½ cup (4 fl oz/118 ml) nut brown ale
2 Tbs unsalted butter
2 Tbs all-purpose flour
½ cup shredded Gruyère cheese
Kosher salt and black pepper

Croque Madame

4 slices of Beer Bread (see page 20)
4 oz (113 g) shaved ham
2 slices Gruyère cheese
2 Tbs unsalted butter
2 eggs

Samuel Smith Nut Brown Ale
(TADCASTER, ENGLAND)
Dundee Ales & Lagers Nut Brown Ale
(ROCHESTER, NY)

Beer-Bread Croque Madame with Beer Mornay Sauce

BEER MORNAY SAUCE

In a small saucepan, melt the butter over medium heat. Add the flour and stir to combine well with the butter. Cook for 1 minute. Add the beer and milk and whisk continuously while bringing to a boil. Once the sauce comes to a boil, remove the pan from the heat. Add the shredded Gruyère and stir to incorporate into the sauce. Season to taste with salt and pepper.

CROQUE MADAME

Preheat a griddle pan over medium heat. Layer the ham and cheese between two slices of beer bread. Add the butter to the preheated pan. Place the sandwiches in the pan and grill 2–3 minutes per side until they are golden brown and the cheese begins to melt. Keep the sandwiches warm while you fry the two eggs to desired doneness.

Place a grilled Croque Madame in the center of each plate. Spoon the desired amount of sauce over the sandwiches. Top each sandwich with 1 fried egg.

Hollandaise

16 Tbs (2 sticks) unsalted butter
¼ cup (2 fl oz/59 ml) American pale ale
3 egg yolks
1 tsp lemon juice + more for seasoning
Kosher salt and black pepper

Benedict

1¼ cup (10 fl oz/296 ml) American pale ale
1 cup (8 fl oz/237 ml) water
2 Tbs (1 fl oz/30 ml) white vinegar
4 eggs
4 slices of good-quality Canadian bacon
2 English muffins, split
Pinch of kosher salt

Sierra Nevada Pale Ale
(CHICO, CA)
3 Floyds Yum Yum or Zombie Dust
(MUNSTER, IN)
Lagunitas New DogTown Pale Ale or
Born Yesterday
(PETALUMA, CA)
Southern Tier Live
(LAKEWOOD, NY)

Pale Ale–Poached Eggs Benedict with Pale Ale Hollandaise Sauce

HOLLANDAISE SAUCE

In a small saucepan over low heat, combine the butter and beer and heat until the butter melts. In a small bowl, combine the egg yolks and 1 teaspoon of lemon juice and whisk for one minute.

To make a double boiler for the hollandaise, fill a small saucepan halfway with water and bring to a simmer over low heat. Rest the bowl with egg yolks on the saucepan. Whisk the egg yolks briskly until they form thick ribbons, about 2–3 minutes. Very slowly drizzle the melted butter and beer mixture into the egg yolks while whisking constantly. Season to taste with salt, pepper, and additional lemon juice. Keep warm until ready to serve.

EGGS BENEDICT

In a shallow saucepan, combine the pale ale, water, and vinegar. Bring to a simmer. Gently crack each egg into a small dish. Add the eggs to the simmering beer one at a time. Poach for 3–5 minutes depending on desired doneness.

While the eggs are poaching, toast the English muffin halves and top each half with a slice of Canadian bacon. Remove the eggs from the simmering beer with a slotted spoon. Let the excess liquid drain off. Top each English muffin half with an egg. Cover with warm Pale Ale Hollandaise Sauce.

ACTIVE PREP: 20 minutes
TOTAL TIME: 30 minutes
SERVES: 4

Pistachio Mousse

2 cup (16 fl oz/473 ml) heavy cream
¼ cup sugar
1 Tbs (½ fl oz/15 ml) vanilla
½ cup pistachio butter

Waffles

2½ cup all-purpose flour
¼ cup sugar
1 Tbs cocoa powder
1 Tbs baking powder
Pinch of kosher salt
2 eggs
1½ cup (12 fl oz/355 ml) imperial stout
1 Tbs (½ fl oz/15 ml) vanilla
4 Tbs (½ stick) unsalted butter, melted

1 oz (28 g) bittersweet chocolate or small block of preferred chocolate

Odell Brewing Lugene
(FORT COLLINS, CO)
Southern Tier 2X Milk Stout
(LAKEWOOD, NY)
Victory Brewing Storm King
(DOWNINGTOWN, PA)

Imperial Stout Waffles with Pistachio Mousse and Chocolate Shavings

PISTACHIO MOUSSE

You can make your own pistachio butter by processing roasted pistachios in a food processor until you have a smooth paste.

In the bowl of a stand mixer, combine the cream, sugar, and vanilla. Beat on high speed until firm peaks form. Add the pistachio butter and beat again just long enough to incorporate. Refrigerate until needed.

WAFFLES

Preheat a waffle iron. In a medium bowl, combine the flour, sugar, cocoa powder, baking powder, and salt and mix well. In a separate large bowl, whisk the eggs, beer, and vanilla. Add the dry ingredients to the beer mixture and stir until mixed. Slowly stir in the melted butter.

Coat the waffle iron with nonstick spray. For the proper amount of batter and cooking time, follow the directions for your specific waffle iron.

Top each hot waffle with a scoop of Pistachio Mousse. Using a fine grater, grate the chocolate over the mousse and waffle.

Breakfast

1 recipe Beer Bread (see page 20), toasted
1 recipe Beer-Glazed Bacon (see page 30)
1 recipe Bourbon-Barrel Stout Breakfast Sausage (see below)
1 recipe Brown Ale Beans (see page 30)
12 eggs
2 ripe tomatoes, sliced

Breakfast Sausage

ACTIVE PREP: 15 minutes
TOTAL TIME: 30 minutes
SERVES: 6–8

¾ cup (6 fl oz/177 ml) bourbon-barrel stout
1 cup ground pork belly or ground pork
1 medium shallot, finely chopped
2 tsp fresh ground pepper
2 tsp Hoppy Cooking hops-infused sea salt
1 tsp nutmeg

Firestone Walker Velvet Merkin
(PASO ROBLES, CA)
Deschutes Brewery The Abyss
(BEND, OR)

Full Irish Breakfast

For the full breakfast, each plate should contain 2 eggs, cooked to order, 1 slice of Beer-Glazed Bacon, 2 patties of Bourbon-Barrel Stout Breakfast Sausage (or 1 slice of the blood pudding, pan-fried), slices of toasted Beer Bread, and Brown Ale Beans. Garnish with sliced tomato.

Bourbon-Barrel Stout Breakfast Sausage

In a large bowl, combine all the ingredients and mix thoroughly by hand. Form the sausage into patties and cook in a medium-hot skillet until fully cooked.

VARIATION

If you are adventurous and would like to try a blood pudding, you'll need 2 cups (16 fl oz/473 ml) of fresh pig's blood and 1 cup of rolled oats. Increase the beer quantity to 1½ cup (12 fl oz/ 355 ml). Preheat the oven to 300°F (149°C). Strain the pig's blood through a fine mesh strainer into a large bowl. Add the remaining ingredients to the bowl and mix thoroughly by hand. Place the mixture in a ceramic terrine or glass loaf pan. Cover tightly with foil and place in the preheated oven. Bake for 60–75 minutes. Remove from the oven and let cool completely. The pudding is best if it is chilled overnight in the refrigerator. To serve, remove the pudding from the pan. Slice into ½-inch slices and pan fry in a little butter.

ACTIVE PREP: 5 minutes
TOTAL TIME: 30 minutes
SERVES: 6–8

1 lb (453 g) thick-sliced bacon
1 cup (8 fl oz/237 ml) red ale or amber ale
½ cup brown sugar
1 Tbs Hoppy Cooking hops-infused sea salt

New Belgium Fat Tire
(FORT COLLINS, CO)

ACTIVE PREP: 35 minutes
TOTAL TIME: 45 minutes
SERVES: 6

1 can of white beans
1 cup (8 fl oz/237 ml) brown ale
2 Tbs (1 fl oz/30 ml) molasses
2 Tbs (1 fl oz/30 ml) tomato paste
1 Tbs sugar
1 tsp garlic powder
Kosher salt and black pepper

Big Sky Brewing Moose Drool
(MISSOULA, MT)
Smuttynose Brewing Old Brown Dog Ale
(HAMPTON, NH)

Beer-Glazed Bacon

Preheat the oven to 375°F (191°C). Line a baking sheet with parchment paper. Separate the bacon slices and lay out in a single layer on the lined baking sheet. In a small bowl, combine the remaining ingredients and mix well. Brush the glaze on the bacon. Place the bacon in the preheated oven. Bake for 25–30 minutes, brushing with the glaze every 7–10 minutes. Remove the bacon from the oven and let it cool before serving.

Note: Hoppy Cooking blends hops with Pacific sea salt to create a salt with citrus and floral notes. Their hops-infused sea salt can be ordered online at hoppycooking.com.

Brown Ale Beans

In a saucepan, combine all the ingredients except the salt and pepper. Bring to a simmer, stirring often. Simmer for 10 minutes. Season to taste with salt and pepper. Reduce the heat and keep warm until ready to serve.

APPETIZERS, SALADS, AND SOUPS

ACTIVE PREP: 20 minutes
TOTAL TIME: 60 minutes
SERVES: 4 as an app, 2 as an entrée

Shrimp

1½ cup (12 fl oz/355 ml) ginger beer
1 cup (8 fl oz/237 ml) water
1 Tbs kosher salt
1 lb (454 g) large shrimp, peeled, deveined, rinsed

Mango Avocado Salad

1 ripe mango
1 avocado, firm when squeezed gently
¼ cup red onion, finely diced
1 Tbs garlic, minced
1 Tbs fresh cilantro, chopped
2 Tbs (1 fl oz/30 ml) fresh lime juice
1 tsp kosher salt
1 tsp ground black pepper

Curry Coconut Cream

1 can (13.5 oz/383 g) coconut cream
Juice of 1 lime or 2 Tbs (1 fl oz/30 ml) fresh lime juice
1 Tbs curry powder
1 Tbs fresh ginger, grated
1 tsp Sriracha sauce or Thai chili paste
1 tsp soy sauce
1 tsp kosher salt
Fresh cilantro for garnish

Fever-Tree Ginger Beer
(LONDON, ENGLAND)
Parker's Ginger Beer
(BOTANY, AUSTRALIA)
Maine Root Ginger Brew
(AUSTIN, TX)

Ginger Beer–Poached Shrimp with Mango Avocado Salad and Curry Coconut Cream

SHRIMP

In a large saucepan, combine the ginger beer, water, and salt. Bring to a simmer. Add the shrimp and simmer 5–6 minutes until the shrimp become pink and opaque. Remove the shrimp from the poaching liquid and place in the refrigerator until thoroughly chilled. Keep the shrimp refrigerated if you're not using them right away.

MANGO AVOCADO SALAD

Halve the mango and the avocado. Scoop out the flesh and dice into ½-inch cubes. Combine all the ingredients in a bowl and mix gently. Taste to check seasoning and adjust if necessary.

CURRY COCONUT CREAM

Coconut cream is much thicker and richer than coconut milk, so be sure to use cream rather than milk when preparing this dish.

In a small bowl, combine all the ingredients except the cilantro and stir or whisk until well combined. It's best to make this sauce a little in advance to give all the flavors time to marry together.

For the plating of this dish, I prefer a square plate, but any plate will be fine. Start by spooning a small pool of the coconut cream in the center of each plate. Stack or fan 3–4 of the chilled shrimp on the cream. Top with a couple of spoonsful of the salad. Drizzle some of the coconut cream over the top and around plate. Garnish with fresh cilantro leaves and Sriracha sauce if desired.

ACTIVE PREP: 45 minutes
TOTAL TIME: 60 minutes
SERVES: 4

Scotch Eggs

6 large eggs (4 for the dish, 2 for the egg wash)
1 cup all-purpose flour
¼ cup (2 fl oz/59 ml) water
1 cup panko bread crumbs
1 cup Italian bread crumbs
8 oz (227 g) ground Italian sausage
1 qt (32 fl oz/946 ml) canola oil for frying
Fresh Italian flat leaf parsley for garnish

Grain-Mustard Sauce

½ cup (4 fl oz/118 ml) whole-grain mustard
¼ cup (2 fl oz/ 59 ml) Wee Heavy–style ale
1 Tbs (½ fl oz/15 ml) honey

AleSmith Wee Heavy Scotch Ale
(SAN DIEGO, CA)
Founders Dirty Bastard
(GRAND RAPIDS, MI)
Thirsty Dog Wulver
(AKRON, OH)
Oskar Blues Old Chub
(LONGMONT, CO)

Scotch Eggs with Wee Heavy Mustard Sauce

SCOTCH EGGS

Hard-boil 4 of the eggs. Cool them and reserve until you need them.

To prepare the eggs, you will need three bowls for your breading station. Place the flour in the first bowl. In the second bowl, whisk together the 2 remaining eggs and the water. In the third bowl, combine the bread crumbs.

Remove the shells from the hard-boiled eggs, being careful to keep the eggs intact. For each egg, you will need about 2 ounces (57 grams) of the Italian sausage. Place the sausage in the palm of your hand and flatten to a patty. Place one hard-boiled egg in the center of the patty. Gently fold the sausage around the egg and pinch closed. Roll the sausage-covered egg around between your hands to smooth. Continue with the remaining eggs.

Dredge the sausage-covered eggs in flour being sure to dust off any excess. Dip the floured eggs in the egg wash, then remove and place in the bread crumbs. Roll the eggs in bread crumbs to coat them thoroughly.

In a deep fryer or large pot, preheat the oil to 325°F (163°C). Slowly lower the breaded eggs into the hot oil. Cook until golden brown and sausage is fully cooked, 4–6 minutes. Remove the eggs from the oil and drain on paper towels. Keep eggs warm while you prepare the Grain-Mustard Sauce.

GRAIN-MUSTARD SAUCE

In a small bowl, combine the three ingredients and stir together.

In the center of each plate, spread a small amount of the grain-mustard sauce. Slice a hot egg in half. Place one half lying with yolk up on the sauce. Lean the remaining half of the egg upright on the already-plated egg. Garnish with fresh parsley and enjoy.

ACTIVE PREP: 15 minutes
TOTAL TIME: 20 minutes
SERVES: 2

1 lb (454 g) fresh mussels, cleaned
1 large shallot, peeled and very thinly sliced
¾ cup (6 fl oz/177 ml) Belgian witbier
1 can (11 oz/312 g) of mandarin orange slices
8–10 basil leaves
4 Tbs cold unsalted butter
Kosher salt
Black pepper

Allagash Brewing White
(PORTLAND, ME)
Avery Brewing White Rascal
(BOULDER, CO)
Alaskan Brewing White
(JUNEAU, AK)

Witbier-Steamed Mussels with Shallots, Orange, and Basil

Preheat a large sauté pan over high heat. Add the mussels, shallot, and beer. Cover and steam for 3–4 minutes. Remove the lid. Add the mandarin orange slices, basil, and butter. Simmer for another 2 minutes to reduce the liquid. Remove from the heat and season to taste with salt and pepper.

Serve the mussels in a large pasta bowl with broth. To serve as an entrée, double the recipe and serve with grilled baguette slices.

ACTIVE PREP: 25 minutes
TOTAL TIME: 35 minutes
SERVES: 2

Frog Legs

3 pair fresh frog legs
1 cup all-purpose flour
1 tsp garlic powder
1 tsp onion powder
1 tsp paprika
1 Tbs kosher salt
1 Tbs black pepper
1½ cup (12 fl oz/355 ml) pale ale
1 cup cornstarch

Gribiche Sauce

1 cup (8 fl oz/237 ml) mayonnaise
¼ cup (2 fl oz/59 ml) Dijon mustard
2 lemons, zested and juiced
2 Tbs capers, chopped
1 Tbs tarragon
Kosher salt
Black pepper

Drake's Brewing 1500
(SAN LEANDRO, CA)
Half Acre Beer Co. Daisy Cutter
(CHICAGO, IL)
Lagunitas Brewing New DogTown
(LAGUNITAS, CA)
Victory Brewing Headwaters
(DOWNINGTOWN, PA)
Southern Tier Brewing Live
(LAKEWOOD, NY)

Beer-Battered Frog Legs with Gribiche Sauce

FROG LEGS

Preheat oil in a deep fryer to 350°F (177°C). Halve the frog legs if they're not already split (slice in between the legs where the thighs meet) and set aside in a shallow baking dish. In a medium bowl, combine the flour and seasonings. Slowly pour in the beer, whisking slowly, adding just enough to make a pancake-batter consistency. Coat the frog legs with cornstarch. Dust off excess. Dip the frog legs in the batter and gently drop into the fryer. Fry for 4–5 minutes until the frog legs are golden brown. Once fully cooked, the frog legs will float to the top. Remove from oil and drain on paper towels.

GRIBICHE SAUCE

In a small bowl, combine the mayonnaise, mustard, lemon zest and juice, capers, and tarragon. Season to taste with salt and pepper.

ACTIVE PREP: 20 minutes
TOTAL TIME: 60 minutes
SERVES: 4

Crisps

2 large beets (or other root vegetable)
¼ cup (2 fl oz/59 ml) extra-virgin olive oil
Kosher salt

Fondue

3 Tbs unsalted butter
2 Tbs all-purpose flour
1 cup (8 fl oz/237 ml) milk
⅔ cup (5.4 fl oz/160 ml) Oktoberfest or
amber beer
1½ cup smoked Gouda, shredded
1½ cup sharp cheddar, shredded
1 tsp Dijon mustard
½ tsp Worcestershire sauce
¼–½ tsp cayenne, to taste
Kosher salt
Black pepper

Jack's Abby Brewing Copper Legend
(FRAMINGHAM, MA)
Great Lakes Brewing Oktoberfest
(CLEVELAND, OH)
New Glarus Staghorn Octoberfest
(NEW GLARUS, WI)
Firestone Walker Brewing Oaktoberfest
(PASO ROBLES, CA)

Root Vegetable Crisps with Beer Cheese Fondue

ROOT VEGETABLE CRISPS

Preheat the oven to 325°F (163°C). Peel the beets with a vegetable peeler and slice very thin, less than $1/12$ inch (2 mm) if possible. You can accomplish this easily with a vegetable mandolin. Line a sheet pan with parchment paper. Toss the beets in the olive oil, making sure that the beets are well coated.

Arrange beets in a single layer on the sheet pan. Brush lightly with olive oil for any beets that might not have been covered. Top with another sheet pan. Bake 20–25 minutes, then carefully remove the top sheet pan. Bake for another 5 minutes. The edges of the beets should begin to curl and brown. Remove from the oven and allow to cool. The beets will crisp up as they cool. Season to taste with salt and serve with Beer Cheese Fondue. The beet chips will keep for 3–4 days.

BEER CHEESE FONDUE

In a large saucepan, melt the butter over medium heat. Whisk in the flour to thicken, taking care not to burn, and then gradually whisk in the milk until the mixture is semi-thick and smooth. Continue whisking while adding the beer. Next, gradually whisk in the cheeses allowing each addition of cheese to melt before adding the next. Once the cheese is melted, whisk in the mustard, Worcestershire sauce, and cayenne pepper. Season to taste with salt and pepper.

ACTIVE PREP: 30 minutes
TOTAL TIME: 45 minutes
SERVES: 4–6

Crust

1 package frozen phyllo dough, thawed
2–3 Tbs (1–1½ fl oz/30–44 ml) extra-virgin olive oil

Filling

2 ripe tomatoes, any variety
2 cup quartered artichoke hearts
1 cup feta cheese
1 clove garlic, thinly sliced
2 Tbs (1 fl oz/30 ml) extra-virgin olive oil
½ tsp crushed red pepper flakes
1 Tbs fresh parsley, chopped
Kosher salt
Black pepper

Tapenade

¾ cup black or green olives
1 clove garlic
2 Tbs (1 fl oz/30 ml) extra-virgin olive oil
2 Tbs (1 fl oz/30 ml) summer-style or light wheat beer
Kosher salt
Black pepper

New Belgium Sunshine Wheat
(**FORT COLLINS, CO**)
Bells Oberon Ale
(**KALAMAZOO, MI**)
Modern Times Fortunate Islands
(**SAN DIEGO, CA**)

Artichoke, Feta, and Tomato Tart with Summer-Ale Tapenade

TART

Preheat the oven to 375°F (191°C). Slice the tomatoes into ¼-inch slices. Place the slices on paper towels to drain while preparing the crust.

For the crust, gently place 1 sheet of phyllo dough in the center of a lightly oiled sheet pan or pie pan. Brush lightly with olive oil. Place a second sheet on top of the first sheet and repeat the process until you have at least 8 layers of dough. Arrange the artichoke hearts in a single layer on top of the phyllo sheets. Be sure to leave at least a 1-inch border around the tart. Place the tomatoes slices neatly on top of the artichokes. Top the tomatoes with sliced garlic. Cover the tart evenly with the feta cheese. Drizzle with olive oil. Sprinkle pepper flakes and parsley on top. Season to taste with salt and pepper. Bake until the feta begins to turn golden brown and the crust is crisp on bottom, 10–12 minutes. Let cool slightly before cutting.

TAPENADE

Combine the olives, garlic, olive oil, and beer in a food processor and pulse in short bursts until the mixture reaches the desired consistency. I prefer mine a bit coarse. You can also make this by mincing the olives and garlic, then whisking all the ingredients together. Check the saltiness before adding salt and pepper as olives tend to be very salty.

To serve, place a portion of the tart on each plate and serve with a spoonful of Summer-Ale Tapenade on the side or on top. Garnish with fresh parsley or even a nice green salad.

ACTIVE PREP: 15 minutes
TOTAL TIME: 50 minutes
SERVES: 4

1 cup (8 fl oz/237 ml) nut brown alèe
8 Tbs (1 stick) unsalted butter
¼ tsp kosher salt
Dash cayenne pepper
1 cup all-purpose flour
5 large eggs
½ cup grated Parmesan cheese
1½ cup grated Swiss cheese
(Emmentaler or Gruyère)
Kosher salt

Rogue Hazelnut Brown Nectar
(NEWPORT, OR)
Big Sky Moose Drool Brown Ale
(MISSOULA, MT)
Sierra Nevada Tumbler Autumn Brown Ale
(CHICO, CA)

Gougères Fait avec Bière (Cheese Puffs Made with Beer)

Preheat the oven to 375°F (191°C). Line 2 cookie sheets with parchment paper.

In a medium saucepan over medium-high heat, bring the beer, butter, ¼ teaspoon of salt, and cayenne pepper just to a boil. Turn off the heat, add all the flour, and stir vigorously with a wooden spoon until a dough forms. Turn the heat back on to medium and continue mixing until the dough dries out, pulls away from the sides of the pan, and forms a smooth ball, 1–2 minutes. Transfer the dough to the bowl of a food processor and let it cool it for 5–6 minutes so it won't cook the eggs when you add them. Process for 5 seconds.

Add the eggs to the dough in the processor bowl. Process until the eggs are well mixed in, about 10–15 seconds. The dough should appear smooth and shiny. Transfer the dough to a bowl and let it cool for 10 minutes.

Set aside 1 tablespoon of the grated Parmesan cheese. Add the remaining Parmesan and the Emmentaler or Gruyére to the dough. Stir with a wooden spoon only enough to incorporate. Don't overmix.

Scoop tablespoon-size mounds onto the parchment-covered cookie sheet, spacing the mounds about 2 inches (5 cm) apart. Sprinkle each mound with a litte salt and a little of the reserved Parmesan cheese. Bake for 30 minutes, or until the gougères are golden brown and crisp.

ACTIVE PREP: 60 minutes
TOTAL TIME: 2 hours
SERVES: 4

8 oz (227 g) chicken livers
1 qt (32 fl oz/946 ml) milk
2 cloves garlic
1 tsp fresh thyme, minced
8 Tbs (1 stick) unsalted butter, chilled
2 egg yolks
¼ cup (2 fl oz/59 ml) Rauchbier
Kosher salt
Black pepper
1 French baguette, sliced
Extra-virgin olive oil
Orange marmalade
Cornichons (small pickled gherkin cucumbers)

Jack's Abby Smoke & Dagger
(FRAMINGHAM, MA)
Fort Collins Brewery Z Lager
(FORT COLLINS, CO)
Ballast Point Abandon Ship Smoked Lager
(SAN DIEGO, CA)

Rauchbier Chicken Liver Pâté with Crostini

The Rauchbier adds a subtle smokiness, giving this pâté lots of depth in flavor.

In a medium bowl, soak the chicken livers in milk for at least 1 hour. Strain, discarding the milk. Combine the livers with the garlic, thyme, butter, egg yolks, and beer in a food processor. Puree until very smooth. Season to taste with salt and pepper.

Preheat the oven to 275°F (135°C). Spread the pate in 4 small ramekins or other mold. Place the ramekins in a roasting pan and fill with hot water to just below the top of each ramekin. Bake for 1 hour. Carefully remove the ramekins from the oven and let cool. Place plastic wrap directly on the pate to prevent a skin from forming. Chill until firm. Serve chilled.

Brush baguette slices with olive oil and bake until golden brown, 5–6 minutes. Serve with pâté, accompanied with a little orange marmalade and cornichons.

ACTIVE PREP: 10 minutes
TOTAL TIME: 10 minutes
SERVES: 4

Raspberry Lambic Dressing

½ cup (4 fl oz/118 ml) raspberry lambic
1 Tbs (½ fl oz/15 ml) Dijon mustard
1 Tbs (½ fl oz/15 ml) honey
1 cup (8 fl oz/237 ml) extra-virgin olive oil
1 Tbs fresh tarragon, minced
Kosher salt
Black pepper

Salad

6–8 oz (170–227 g) organic baby spinach leaves
1 medium red onion, very thinly sliced
4 oz (113 g) goat cheese
1 pint fresh raspberries

Oud Beersel Framboise
(BEERSEL, BELGIUM)
Odell Brewing Friek
(FORT COLLINS, CO)
Upland Brewing Raspberry Lambic
(BLOOMINGTON, IN)

Spinach Salad with Goat Cheese and Raspberry Lambic Dressing

RASPBERRY LAMBIC DRESSING

In a small bowl, combine the lambic, mustard, and honey and mix thoroughly. Slowly add the olive oil while whisking continuously. Add the fresh tarragon. Season to taste with salt and pepper.

SALAD

Fill 4 salad bowls with the spinach leaves. Top with the sliced onion, crumbled goat cheese, and raspberries. Spoon the dressing over the salad.

ACTIVE PREP: 15 minutes
TOTAL TIME: 20 minutes
SERVES: 4

Salad

2 hearts of romaine lettuce
4 strips of bacon, cooked and chopped, reserving 1 Tbs (½ fl oz/15 ml) of bacon drippings for the vinaigrette
4 oz (113 g) bleu cheese, crumbled

Vinaigrette

½ cup (4 fl oz/118 ml) Hefeweizen beer
1 Tbs (½ fl oz/15 ml) sherry vinegar
1 Tbs orange zest
1 tsp lemon zest
1 tsp rosemary, finely chopped
1 cup (8 fl oz/237 ml) extra-virgin olive oil
1 Tbs (½ fl oz/15 ml) reserved bacon drippings

Kosher salt
Black pepper

Sierra Nevada Kellerweis Hefeweizen
(CHICO, CA)
Tröegs DreamWeaver Wheat
(HERSHEY, PA)
Victory Winter Cheers
(DOWNINGTOWN, PA)

Grilled Romaine Hearts with Bacon, Bleu Cheese, and Citrus Hefeweizen Vinaigrette

SALAD

Preheat a grill or grill pan on medium-high heat. Cut each romaine heart in half lengthwise. Grill cut side down for 1–2 minutes until slightly charred.

VINAIGRETTE

In a small bowl, combine the beer, vinegar, orange and lemon zest, and rosemary. Slowly add the olive oil, then bacon drippings while whisking constantly. Season to taste with salt and pepper.

To plate, place 1 grilled romaine heart in the center of each plate. Top with the chopped bacon and crumbled bleu cheese. Spoon the Citrus Hefeweizen Vinaigrette over the salad and around the plate. If you don't like bleu cheese, you can substitute feta. You could also add orange segments to the salad for more citrus flavor.

Bisque

2 Tbs unsalted butter
1 lb (454 g) parsnips, peeled and diced
1 large shallot, peeled and minced
1½ cup (12 fl oz/355 ml) hard cider
1 cup (8 fl oz/237 ml) heavy cream
1 Tbs fresh thyme
1 Tbs kosher salt
1 tsp white pepper

Croutons

2 thick slices of sourdough bread
2 Tbs (1 fl oz/30 ml) extra-virgin olive oil
1 Tbs (½ fl oz/15 ml) walnut oil
1 clove garlic, minced to a paste consistency
1 tsp kosher salt

Virtue Cider RedStreak
(FENNVILLE, MI)
Foggy Ridge Serious Cider
(DUGSPUR, VA)
Square Mile Spur & Vine
(PORTLAND, OR)

Hard Cider Parsnip Bisque with Sourdough Croutons

BISQUE

In a heavy saucepan, heat the butter over medium-high. Add the parsnips and shallot. Sweat for 3–4 minutes, stirring frequently. Add the hard cider, making sure the parsnips are completely covered (more cider may be necessary depending on the size of pan). Simmer 12–15 minutes until the parsnips become tender. Add the heavy cream, thyme, salt, and pepper. Simmer an additional 2–3 minutes. Remove from the heat. Place mixture in blender and puree until smooth.

CROUTONS

Preheat the oven to 350°F (177°C). Cut the bread slices into ½-inch (13-mm) cubes. In a medium bowl, combine the remaining ingredients, then add the croutons and mix to coat the croutons thoroughly. Spread the croutons evenly on a sheet pan and bake for 8–10 minutes or until golden brown.

ACTIVE PREP: 25 minutes
TOTAL TIME: 35 minutes
SERVES: 4

2 large white onions
4 Tbs (½ stick) unsalted butter
2 cloves garlic, sliced
1 bay leaf
1 Tbs fresh thyme, chopped
1½ cup (12 fl oz/355 ml) dry Irish stout
1 qt (32 fl oz/946 ml) unsalted beef broth
Kosher salt
Black pepper
4 thick slices of sourdough or French bread
8 slices of Gruyère cheese

Alaskan Stout
(JUNEAU, AK)
Victory Brewing Donnybrook Stout
(DOWNINGTOWN, PA)
Moylan's Dragoons Stout
(NOVATO, CA)
O'Hara's Irish Stout
(COUNTY CARLOW, IRELAND)

Irish Stout Onion Soup with Gruyère Crouton

Peel and slice the onions into ⅛-inch (3-mm) slices (a julienne cut). In a large heavy-bottom pan over medium heat, melt the butter. Add the onions and cook slowly for 25–30 minutes, stirring often until they reach a dark caramel color. Add the garlic, bay leaf, and thyme to the pan. Add the beer to the pan and bring to a boil. Add the beef broth and reduce heat to a simmer. Simmer for 10 minutes. Season to taste with salt and pepper.

Arrange 4 ovenproof soup bowls on a sheet pan. Ladle the soup into the bowls. Lay a slice of bread on top of each bowl of soup. Top evenly with cheese. Place the sheet pan carefully under a preheated broiler on high setting. Broil until bubbling and browned.

ACTIVE PREP: 90 minutes
TOTAL TIME: 2 hours
SERVES: 4

Empanadas

1 whole beef tongue
Extra-virgin olive oil
2 qt (64 fl oz/1.9 l) beef stock
8 oz (227 g) Cotija cheese
2–3 green onions, thinly sliced white portion (save the greens for garnish later)
Kosher salt
Black pepper
1 package of frozen puff pastry, thawed

Beef Tongue Empanadas with Cotija Cheese, Fig Jam, Candied Pecans, and Apricot Ale Glaze

EMPANADAS

In a heavy-bottom pan, deep enough to fit the tongue, brown the beef tongue in a little oil over medium-high heat. Once the tongue is browned on all sides, add the beef stock and bring to a boil. Reduce the heat to a very low simmer and cover tightly. Simmer for about 90 minutes, maybe longer depending on the size of the tongue. The meat should be fork tender. Remove from the pan and let cool for at least 30 minutes. Peel the outer layer of tongue off and discard. Shred the remaining meat with a fork.

Preheat the oven to 400°F (204°C). Line a sheet pan with parchment paper. In a medium bowl, combine the shredded meat, Cotija, and green onions. Season to taste with salt and pepper. Reserve mixture until ready to form empanadas. Unfold the thawed puff pastry sheet on a lightly floured work surface. Cut out eight 4-inch diameter circles. Prick each with a fork several times. Flip the puff pastry circles over (fork holes should be on the outside) and place a spoonful of filling in the center of each circle of pastry. Fold over and crimp edges with a fork to seal tightly. Place the empanadas on the parchment-lined sheet pan and bake for 12–15 minutes until golden brown.

Fig Jam
1 cup dried figs
1 cup (8 fl oz/237 ml) lambic

Apricot Ale Glaze
1½ cup (12 fl oz/355 ml) apricot ale
¼ cup (2 fl oz/59 ml) honey
1 Tbs (½ fl oz/15 ml) red wine vinegar

Candied Pecans
2 Tbs unsalted butter, melted
¼ cup brown sugar
1 tsp cinnamon
½ tsp ground ginger
Pinch of cayenne pepper
1 cup pecan pieces

For the fig jam
New Belgium Transatiantique Kriek
(FORT COLLINS, CO)
Allagash Coolship Red
(PORTLAND, ME)
Brasserie Cantillon Kriek 100% Lambic
(ANDERLECHT, BELGIUM)

For the glaze
Dry Dock Apricot Blonde
(AURORA, CO)
Samuel Smith Organic Apricot Ale
(TADCASTER, ENGLAND)

FIG JAM
In a small saucepan, combine the figs and beer and bring to a boil. Remove from the heat and let the fig mixture cool completely. Once cooled, puree the mixture in a food processor. Reserve for plating.

APRICOT ALE GLAZE
In a small saucepan, combine all the ingredients and bring to a low boil. Reduce by about half in volume or until thick and syrupy.

CANDIED PECANS
Preheat the oven to 325°F (163°C). In a medium bowl, mix the butter, brown sugar, and spices together. Add the pecan pieces and stir to coat well. Spread the mixture on a sheet pan and bake for 10–12 minutes.

To serve, arrange 2 empanadas on each plate, one leaning on the other. Place a spoonful of Fig Jam near the empanadas and drizzle the Apricot Ale Glaze over the top. Sprinkle Candied Pecan pieces around the plate. Garnish with reserved greens from the green onions.

FISH AND SHELLFISH

ACTIVE PREP: 20 minutes
TOTAL TIME: 70–85 minutes
SERVES: 4

Beer-Cheese Grits

3 cup (24 fl oz/710 ml) water
1 cup (8 fl oz/237 ml) brown ale
½ cup (4 fl oz/118 ml) milk or cream
1 cup coarse-ground white grits
1 cup shredded smoked Gouda
Kosher salt
Black pepper

Shrimp

4 Tbs (2 fl oz/59 ml) extra-virgin olive oil
4–6 cloves garlic, minced
1 green bell pepper, julienned
1 red bell pepper, julienned
1 red onion, julienned
1 lb (454 g) shrimp, peeled and deveined
2 Tbs blackening or Creole spice
1 tsp all-purpose flour
½ cup diced tomatoes
1 cup (8 fl oz/237 ml) lager
8 Tbs (1 stick) unsalted butter
Kosher salt
Black pepper

New Belgium Brewing Blue Paddle
(FORT COLLINS, CO)
Firestone Walker Pivo Pils
(PASO ROBLES, CA)
August Schell's Pils
(NEW ULM, MN)

Sautéed Shrimp and Beer-Cheese Grits with Creole Lager Sauce

BEER-CHEESE GRITS

In a medium saucepan, bring the water, beer, and milk to a boil. Slowly whisk in the grits. Continue whisking slowly for at least 1 minute. Reduce the heat to low and cover. Simmer for 45–60 minutes whisking often so the grits don't stick to bottom of the pan. Remove from the heat and stir in the cheese. Season to taste with salt and pepper.

SHRIMP

Heat a large skillet or sauté pan over medium-high heat. Add the olive oil and garlic. Cook the garlic for 1–2 minutes. Add the bell peppers and onion and continue cooking 5–7 minutes, stirring occasionally. Add the shrimp, blackening spice, and flour to pan. Stir well to coat everything in spices. Cook an additional 2 minutes, then add the tomatoes, lager, and butter. Bring the sauce to a boil, then reduce heat to low. Simmer for 7–10 minutes to thicken the sauce. Season to taste with salt and pepper.

Spoon the Beer-Cheese Grits into the center of each large pasta bowl. Arrange the shrimp, peppers, and onion on top of the grits. Cover with the lager sauce left in the pan.

ACTIVE PREP: 20 minutes
TOTAL TIME: 30 minutes
SERVES: 2

Glaze

¾ cup (6 fl oz/177 ml) amber/red ale
½ cup light brown sugar
1 Tbs (½ fl oz/15 ml) Dijon mustard
1 Tbs (½ fl oz/15 ml) apple cider vinegar
1 Tbs (½ fl oz/15 ml) tomato paste

Hash

1 cup fresh Brussels sprouts, split in half
2 Tbs (1 fl oz/30 ml) extra-virgin olive oil
2 Tbs unsalted butter
1 medium sweet potato, peeled and cut in ½" diced
1 large shallot, sliced
2 Tbs garlic, minced
¾ cup (6 fl oz/177 ml) amber/red ale
½ cup (4 fl oz/118 ml) water
1 Tbs fresh thyme
Kosher salt
Black pepper

Salmon

Two 6–8 oz (170–227 g) salmon steaks

New Belgium Fat Tire
(FORT COLLINS, CO)
Tröegs Nugget Nectar
(HERSHEY, PA)
Brewery Ommegang Fire and Blood Red Ale
(COOPERSTOWN, NY)

Amber-Ale Glazed Salmon with Roasted Brussels Sprouts and Sweet Potato Hash

GLAZE

In a small bowl, mix all the ingredients together until well combined. You can make the glaze up to 24 hours in advance and refrigerate until needed.

HASH

Preheat the oven to 400°F (204°C). In a small bowl, toss the Brussels sprouts with the olive oil and a pinch of salt and pepper. Spread on a sheet pan and roast for 8–10 minutes or until the Brussels sprouts just begin to brown. Remove from the oven and set aside.

In a heavy sauté pan, heat the butter over medium heat. Add the sweet potato, shallot, and garlic. Sauté for 3–4 minutes until the sweet potato begins to soften around the edges just a bit. Add the beer, water, and thyme. Keep the liquid at a simmer for 8–10 minutes, stirring frequently. Add the Brussels sprouts and continue to simmer until the liquid is completely absorbed and the sweet potato is tender. If you need more liquid before the sweet potato is fully cooked, use water. Season to taste with salt and pepper.

SALMON

Preheat a grill or grill pan over medium-high heat. Coat the grill with nonstick spray. Place the salmon steaks on the grill at a 45° angle. Grill 3–4 minutes on the first side. Flip. Baste the salmon liberally with the glaze. Grill an additional 3–4 minutes, basting as necessary to achieve the desired glaze amount. Be aware of flare-ups, as the glaze will burn due to the high sugar content.

Spoon the Sweet Potato Hash into the center of each dinner plate. Top each mound of hash with a salmon steak. Drizzle the plates with a little of the remaining Amber-Ale Glaze.

ACTIVE PREP: 25 minutes
TOTAL TIME: 35 minutes
SERVES: 2

Beans

1½ cup frozen fava or lima beans
1 large shallot, thinly sliced
2 Tbs unsalted butter
2 Tbs garlic, minced
1 Tbs fresh thyme, chopped
Kosher salt
Black pepper

Hefeweizen Beurre Blanc

1 cup (8 fl oz/237 ml) Hefeweizen
1 large shallot, chopped
2 sprigs fresh thyme
16 Tbs (2 sticks) unsalted butter, cubed
and kept cold
Kosher salt
Black pepper

Halibut

2 Tbs unsalted butter
1 Tbs (½ fl oz/15 ml) vegetable/canola oil
12–14 oz (340–397 g) fresh halibut
cheeks or filets
Kosher salt
Black pepper
1 lemon, cut in half
Lemon wedges
Fresh thyme sprigs

Sierra Nevada Kellerweis Hefeweizen
(CHICO, CA)
Tröegs DreamWeaver Wheat
(HERSHEY, PA)

Pan-Roasted Halibut Cheeks with Fava Beans and Hefeweizen Beurre Blanc

BEANS

Place the beans in a small saucepan and cover with water. Bring to a boil and cook for 3–4 minutes. Pour the beans into a strainer. Using the same pot, melt the butter, add the shallot and garlic and sauté until tender. Add the cooked beans and the thyme. Season to taste with salt and pepper. Keep warm until ready to plate.

HEFEWEISEN BEURRE BLANC

In a small saucepan, bring the beer, shallot, and thyme to a boil and reduce the mixture until you have about ¼ cup (2 fl oz/59 ml) left. Reduce the heat to low. Slowly whisk in the butter a few cubes at a time. Once you have incorporated half the butter, remove the mixture from the heat and whisk in the remaining butter. Season to taste with salt and pepper.

HALIBUT

Heat a heavy-bottom sauté pan over medium-high heat. Add the butter and oil. Season the halibut with salt and pepper. Gently place the halibut cheeks in the sauté pan. Sear for 4–5 minutes without moving. Once the fish has developed a nice golden crust, flip the pieces over and continue cooking for another 4–5 minutes using a large spoon to baste the halibut with the browning butter in the pan. Turn off the heat. Squeeze lemon juice over the top and baste some more.

Spoon a mound of fava/lima beans in the center of each large pasta bowl. Place halibut cheeks on top of the beans. Fill the bowl around the beans with the Hefeweisen Beurre Blanc. Garnish each bowl with lemon slices and a sprig of thyme.

ACTIVE PREP: 25 minutes
TOTAL TIME: 45 minutes
SERVES: 4

Black-eyed Pea Cakes

1 slice bacon
½ onion, chopped
4 cloves garlic, minced
Extra-virgin olive oil
Two 15.8 oz (448 g) cans of black-eyed
peas, drained
1 Tbs fresh cilantro
½ tsp cumin
½ tsp cayenne
1½ tsp kosher salt
2 eggs, beaten
2 cup panko or bread crumbs
Kosher salt
Black pepper

Barbeque Sauce

½ cup (4 fl oz/118 ml) farmhouse-style ale
½ cup (4 fl oz/118 ml) ketchup
¼ cup brown sugar
1 clove garlic, minced
2 Tbs (1 fl oz/30 ml) apple cider vinegar
1 Tbs smoked paprika
1 tsp chili powder

Swordfish

4 swordfish steaks, 6–8 oz (170–227 g) each
Kosher salt
Black pepper
2 oz (57 g) crème fraiche

Boulevard Tank 7
(KANSAS CITY, MO)
Perennial Artisan Ales Saison de Lis
(ST. LOUIS, MO)

Barbecued Swordfish Steak with Black-eyed Pea Cakes

BLACK-EYED PEA CAKES

In a small sauté pan, sauté the bacon, onion, and garlic in about 2 tablespoons of olive oil until softened. In a food processor, combine half of the black-eyed peas, the bacon mixture, cilantro, cumin, cayenne, and salt; pulse a few times until blended (it doesn't need to be totally smooth). Transfer the mixture to a medium bowl and stir in the remaining black-eyed peas, eggs, and bread crumbs. Season to taste with salt and pepper. Chill the mixture until it is cool enough to handle, about an hour, then gently form it into cakes and set aside.

Line a plate or cooling rack with paper towels. In a large skillet over medium heat, heat 3–4 tablespoons of olive oil. In small batches, add the black-eyed pea cakes to the skillet. Cook about 2–3 minutes on each side until they are golden brown. Watch the oil for overheating, and, if needed, add more oil or start with new oil if it gets too dark. Remove the cakes and let them cool on the paper-towel lined plate or rack.

BARBEQUE SAUCE

In a small bowl, whisk together the ale, ketchup, brown sugar, garlic, vinegar, paprika, and chili powder.

SWORDFISH

Preheat a grill on high heat. Season the swordfish steaks with salt and pepper and place them on the grill. Grill on the first side for 4–5 minutes. Turn the steaks and brush with the barbecue sauce. Continue grilling for another 3–4 minutes. Turn the fish again and brush with sauce. Finish cooking for another minute or so. Turn once again and brush the tops of the steaks with sauce a final time and remove from the grill.

Serve each swordfish steak accompanied with Black-Eyed Pea Cakes topped with a spoonful of crème fraiche.

ACTIVE PREP: 20 minutes
TOTAL TIME: 35 minutes
SERVES: 4–6

2 shallots, minced
8 Tbs (1 stick) unsalted butter
¼ cup all-purpose flour
1 qt (32 fl oz/946 ml) milk
1½ cup (12 fl oz/355 ml) pale ale
½ tsp ground nutmeg
1 Tbs fresh thyme, chopped
Kosher salt
Black pepper
3 cup shredded cheddar cheese
1 lb (454 g) elbow macaroni, cooked and rinsed
12–16 oz (340–454 g) lobster meat, roughly chopped
1 cup grated Parmesan cheese

Sierra Nevada Pale Ale
(CHICO, CA)
3 Floyds Zombie Dust
(MUNSTER, IN)
Lagunitas New DogTown Pale Ale
(PETALUMA, CA)
Southern Tier Live
(LAKEWOOD, NY)

American Pale Ale Lobster Mac-N-Cheese

In a heavy-bottom saucepan over low heat, sweat the shallots in the butter for 5–6 minutes. Stir in the flour and continue cooking for another 2 minutes or so. Add the milk and the beer and bring to a boil, whisking the entire time. Make sure there are no lumps from the roux mixture left in the sauce. Reduce the heat to low and cook for 20 minutes. Remove from the heat. Add the nutmeg and thyme and season to taste with salt and pepper. Whisk in the cheddar.

Preheat the oven to 350°F (177°C). In a large bowl, mix the macaroni with the cheese sauce. Fold in the lobster meat and transfer to a baking dish. Top with the Parmesan cheese and bake for about 15 minutes or until the cheese is golden brown.

Serve as an entrée with a fresh green salad or as a side dish with beef tenderloin.

ACTIVE PREP: 20 minutes
TOTAL TIME: 35 minutes
SERVES: 4

Flounder

1 medium green bell pepper, minced
1 medium yellow onion, minced
4 cloves garlic, minced
1 stalk celery, minced
2 Tbs unsalted butter
¼ cup (2 fl oz/59 ml) mayonnaise
Juice of 1 lemon
1 Tbs fresh parsley
1 Tbs fresh tarragon (optional)
1 cup lump crab meat
¼ cup Parmesan cheese, grated
4 flounder filets
Kosher salt
Black pepper
1 recipe Beer-Cheese Grits (page 62) made with 2 cups shredded cheddar or Gouda

Grilled Spring Onions

1 bunch spring (green) onions
2 Tbs (1 fl oz/30 ml) extra virgin olive oil

Big Sky Brewing Moose Drool
(MISSOULA, MT)

Upslope Brewing Brown Ale
(BOULDER, CO)

Crab-Stuffed Flounder with Beer-Cheese Grits and Grilled Spring Onions

FLOUNDER

In a medium pan, sauté the green pepper, onion, garlic, and celery in the butter until the vegetables are tender. Remove from the heat and let cool. While the vegetables are cooling, in a medium bowl, combine the mayonnaise, lemon juice, parsley, and tarragon. Add the vegetable mixture. Gently fold in the crab and Parmesan until just combined.

Preheat the oven to 400°F (204°C). Butter a large baking dish. Arrange the flounder filets on a work surface. Season with salt and pepper. Evenly distribute the crab mixture among the filets, then roll up the filets, jelly-roll style. Arrange the rolls in the baking dish. Bake for 12–15 minutes, until the crab stuffing begins to brown.

GRILLED SPRING ONIONS

Preheat a grill or grill pan on medium-high heat. Trim the root end of the spring onions and cut the green part off about 1 inch (25 mm) above the white part. Reserve the greens for another use. Toss the onions with the olive oil and grill until charred lightly.

Mound the grits on each plate. Top each mound with a flounder filet roll and garnish with the Grilled Spring Onions.

ACTIVE PREP: 25 minutes
TOTAL TIME: 90 minutes
SERVES: 4

Corn Pudding

2 cup fresh corn kernels
½ cup (4 fl oz/118 ml) rye beer
½ cup (4 fl oz/118 ml) heavy cream
2 eggs
4 egg yolks
2 Tbs sugar
2 Tbs all-purpose flour
½ tsp baking powder
Kosher salt
Black pepper

Chimichurri

¼ cup fresh parsley, coarsely chopped
3 Tbs (1½ fl oz/44 ml) lemon juice
4 large cloves garlic, minced
1 tsp oregano leaves
1 tsp crushed red pepper
½ cup (4 fl oz/118 ml) extra-virgin olive oil
Kosher salt
Black pepper

Trout

4 whole trout, butterflied and deboned
Kosher salt
Black pepper
2 Tbs cornstarch
4 slices bacon

Founders Red's Rye IPA
(GRAND RAPIDS, MI)
Two Brothers Brewing Cane & Ebel
(WARRENVILLE, IL)
Boulevard Brewing Rye-on-Rye
(KANSAS CITY, MO)

Bacon-Wrapped Trout with Rye Beer Corn Pudding and Chimichurri

CORN PUDDING

Preheat the oven to 300°F (149°C). Butter 4 ramekins. In a blender, combine the corn, beer, and cream. Puree until smooth. Add the eggs, egg yolks, sugar, flour, and baking powder and blend for another 30 seconds. Divide the mixture evenly among the buttered ramekins. Place the ramekins in a baking dish. Fill the baking dish with about 1 inch (2.5 cm) of hot water. Cover tightly with foil and bake for 60–90 minutes. The center of the puddings should be set and a bit wobbly but not runny. Carefully remove from the oven and let cool slightly before removing from the water bath. These puddings are best served warm, so reheat after you prepare the trout.

CHIMICHURRI

In a blender, combine the parsley, lemon juice, garlic, oregano, red pepper, and olive oil. Blend for 30 seconds to 1 minute until well combined. Season to taste with salt and pepper.

TROUT

Preheat the oven to 400°F (204°C). Season the trout with salt and pepper. Lightly dust the trout skin with cornstarch and shake off any excess. Fold trout in half with the flesh side in. Wrap each trout with a piece of bacon, stretching the bacon gently. Be sure to have both ends of the bacon slice under the trout. Place the bacon-wrapped trout on a sheet pan. Bake for 10–12 minutes, then turn and cook for another 6–8 minutes. Bacon and skin should be crispy and browned.

Unmold each corn pudding onto a plate. Place a trout on each plate and garnish with Chimichurri sauce.

ACTIVE PREP: 25 minutes
TOTAL TIME: 40 minutes
SERVES: 2

Cauliflower

1 head of cauliflower, florets separated
1 tsp curry powder
2 cup (16 fl oz/473 ml) whole milk
1 large shallot
Kosher salt
Black pepper

Harissa Oil

2 Tbs Harissa paste
¼ cup (2 fl oz/59 ml) extra-virgin olive oil

Scallops

6–8 jumbo sea scallops (U10)
Kosher salt
Black pepper
2 Tbs (1 fl oz/30 ml) extra-virgin olive oil
½ cup (4 fl oz/118 ml) India pale ale
8 Tbs (1 stick) unsalted butter
1 bay leaf
3 cloves garlic, whole

Charred Lemon

1 lemon, cut in to ¼" slices

Garnish

Fresh parsley, chopped

Firestone Walker Union Jack IPA
(PASO ROBLES, CA)
Samuel Adams Rebel IPA
(BOSTON, MA)
Odell IPA
(FORT COLLINS, CO)

Butter and Beer-Poached Sea Scallops with Curried Cauliflower

CAULIFLOWER

In a large saucepan, combine the cauliflower florets, curry powder, milk, and shallot. Bring to a boil. Reduce the heat and simmer for 7–10 minutes until the cauliflower is tender. Remove from the heat. Reserve 8–10 florets. Place the remaining mixture in a blender and puree to the desired smoothness. Season to taste with salt and pepper. Keep warm until ready to serve.

HARISSA OIL

In a small bowl, mix the harissa paste into the olive oil. Place the mixture in a squeeze bottle if you have one (a spoon will do fine if you don't).

SCALLOPS

Season the scallops with salt and pepper. In a wide saucepan over medium-high heat, heat the olive oil. Carefully place scallops in the hot oil. Sear for 2 minutes. Turn the scallops over and add all remaining ingredients. Bring to a boil. Cover and turn off the heat. Let sit until ready to serve.

CHARRED LEMON

Grill the lemon slices until they begin to char. You can also do this under a broiler in the oven.

Spoon the curried cauliflower puree into the center of each plate. Using the back of the spoon, spread the puree around evenly. Place 3–4 scallops in a triangle on top of the puree on each plate. Arrange 4–5 reserved cauliflower florets on each plate. Top scallops with Charred Lemon slices. Drizzle the scallops and plates with the Harissa Oil. Garnish with fresh chopped parsley.

ACTIVE PREP: 15 minutes
TOTAL TIME: 25 minutes
SERVES: 2

Cioppino

2 Tbs unsalted butter, divided

3 Tbs garlic, minced

1 lb (454 g) shrimp, peeled, deveined, and rinsed

1 lb (454 g) fresh mussels

1 lb (454 g) fresh clams, manila or littleneck

1½ cup (12 fl oz/355 ml) San Francisco–style Steam Beer

14.5 oz (411 g) can diced tomatoes, drained

8 oz (227 g) lump crab meat

1 Tbs fresh thyme, chopped

1 Tbs fresh oregano, chopped

Kosher salt

Black pepper

Grilled Bread

4 thick slices of French baguette

2 Tbs extra-virgin olive oil

Anchor Steam
(SAN FRANCISCO, CA)

Jack's Abby Steam Pie
(BOSTON, MA)

New Belgium California Route
(FORT COLLINS, CO)

Steamworks Steam Engine Lager
(DURANGO, CO)

Steam Beer Shellfish Cioppino with Grilled Bread

CIOPPINO

Heat a large sauté pan over medium heat. Add 1 tablespoon butter and the garlic. Sauté for 1–2 minutes, being careful to not let the butter brown too much. Add the shrimp, mussels, and clams and increase the heat to high. Pour in the beer and tomatoes. Cover and steam for 2–3 minutes. Carefully remove the lid. Add the crab, remaining tablespoon of butter, and herbs and continue to boil for 2–3 minutes. Remove from the heat. Season to taste with salt and pepper.

GRILLED BREAD

Preheat a grill or cast-iron grill pan on medium-high heat. Brush one side of the bread slices with oil and place them on the grill oil side down. Grill for about 1 minute, or until the bread has begun to char slightly.

Ladle the cioppino into large pasta bowls. Serve the bread on the side.

ACTIVE PREP: 25 minutes
TOTAL TIME: 30 minutes
SERVES: 4

Lager-Lime Vinaigrette

¼ cup (2 fl oz/59 ml) Mexican lager
1 lime, juiced
2 Tbs (1 fl oz/30 ml) agave syrup
¾ cup (6 fl oz/177 ml) extra-virgin olive oil
1 tsp kosher salt
1 tsp black pepper

Prawns

24 prawns, peeled, deveined, and rinsed
½ cup (4 fl oz/118 ml) agave syrup
1 lime, zested and juiced
2 Tbs garlic, minced
2 Tbs (1 fl oz/30 ml) extra-virgin olive oil
Kosher salt
Black pepper

Corn Salad

3 large ears of sweet corn, cleaned
1 red onion, diced
2 cloves garlic, minced
2 limes, zested and juiced
½ cup cream cheese
1 Tbs fresh cilantro, finely chopped
Kosher salt
Black pepper

Ska Brewing Mexican Logger
(DURANGO, CO)
Big Wood Brewery Amigo Grande
(WHITE BEAR LAKE, MN)

Glazed Prawns with Grilled Corn Salad and Lager-Lime Vinaigrette

LAGER-LIME VINAIGRETTE
In a small bowl, combine all the ingredients and whisk together for about 1 minute. Set aside.

PRAWNS
In a large bowl, combine the prawns, agave syrup, lime zest and juice, garlic, and olive oil. Mix thoroughly and season to taste with salt and pepper. Marinate for 10–30 minutes. While the prawns are marinating, prepare the Corn Salad.

Preheat the grill to medium-high heat. Spray the grill with nonstick spray. Remove the prawns from the marinade and place them on the grill. Grill for 2–3 minutes on each side. Brush the prawns with the marinade after turning. The prawns will become bright pink and opaque when they are fully cooked.

CORN SALAD
Preheat a grill to medium-high heat. Place the corn ears on the hot grill. While the corn is cooking, in a large bowl, combine the onion, garlic, lime zest and juice, and cream cheese. Mix well. Grill the corn until the kernels begin to blacken. Using a sharp knife, slice the corn kernels off the ear and into the bowl with the cream-cheese mixture. Season to taste with salt and pepper and mix well.

To plate, mound the Grilled Corn Salad in the center of each plate. Arrange 6 prawns on top of each mound. Spoon the Lager-Lime Vinaigrette over the prawns and around the plates. If desired, garnish each plate with fresh cilantro leaves and a lime wedge.

ACTIVE PREP: 30 minutes
TOTAL TIME: 50 minutes
SERVES: 2

Tomato Jam
One 10–12 oz (284–340 g) can diced tomatoes, undrained
2 Tbs sugar
1 Tbs smoked paprika
¼ tsp cayenne pepper
Kosher salt
Black pepper

Tilapia En Croute
2 cup wild mushrooms, such as shiitake, cremini, or oyster, rough-chopped
1 large shallot, minced
2 Tbs garlic, minced
1 Tbs fresh thyme, minced
1 Tbs fresh tarragon, minced
¼ cup (2 fl oz/59 ml) extra-virgin olive oil
½ cup (4 fl oz/118 ml) dry sherry
1 sheet of puff pastry dough
2 large tilapia filets
Kosher salt
Black pepper
1 egg, beaten

Fondue
½ cup (4 fl oz/118 ml) imperial white ale
4–6 oz (113–170 g) mascarpone cheese
Kosher salt

Garnish
Fresh thyme
Tarragon

Samuel Adams Imperial White
(BOSTON, MA)

Wild Mushroom and Tilapia En Croute with Ale-Mascarpone Fondue

TOMATO JAM *(Recipe will make extra)*
In a small saucepan, combine the diced tomatoes, sugar, paprika, and cayenne pepper and bring to a simmer. Simmer 30–45 minutes, stirring occasionally, until thickened. Season to taste with salt and pepper.

TILAPIA EN CROUTE
In a large sauté pan, sauté the mushrooms, shallot, garlic, and herbs in olive oil. When the mushrooms start to caramelize, deglaze the pan with the dry sherry and cook until dry.

Preheat the oven to 400°F (204°C). Line a sheet pan with parchment paper. Cut the puff pastry into 4 pieces about 1 inch (25 mm) larger than the tilapia filets on all sides. Place 2 puff pastry sheets on the parchment-lined sheet pan. Place 1 filet on each pastry sheet. Season well with salt and pepper. Top each filet with half of the mushroom mixture. Brush the edges of the puff pastry with the beaten egg. Lay the second pastry sheet over each filet and press the edges together firmly to seal. Brush the top with the egg and cut 3 small slits in pastry. Bake until the puff pastry is a deep golden brown, about 10–12 minutes.

FONDUE
While the tilapia bakes, in a small saucepan, bring the ale to a simmer and reduce by half. Remove from the heat and let cool to room temperature or a little warmer. Add the mascarpone and whisk slowly until it is completely incorporated. Season to taste with salt.

Ladle the fondue onto 2 large dinner plates. Place 1 Tilapia en Croute in the center of each plate. Top each tilapia with a large spoonful of the Tomato Jam. Garnish with fresh herbs.

POULTRY AND MEAT

ACTIVE PREP: 20 minutes
TOTAL TIME: 90 minutes
SERVES: 2–4

Chicken

1 whole organic chicken, washed and dried
Kosher salt
Black pepper

Butter

16 Tbs (2 sticks) unsalted butter, softened
1 cup (8 fl oz/237 ml) India pale ale
1 large shallot, minced
2 Tbs garlic, minced
1 Tbs fresh parsley, chopped
1 tsp fresh thyme, chopped
Zest of 1 lemon
1 Tbs kosher salt

Firestone Walker Union Jack IPA
(PASO ROBLES, CA)
Samuel Adams Rebel IPA
(BOSTON, MA)
Odell IPA
(FORT COLLINS, CO)
Ska Modus Hoperandi IPA
(DURANGO, CO)

Simple Roast Chicken Rubbed with IPA Butter

Preheat the oven to 450°F (232°C).

In the bowl of a food processor, combine the butter with the other ingredients. Pulse until well combined.

Place the chicken in a heavy roasting pan. Rub the butter all over the chicken, including under the skin. Fold the wings under the chicken and tie the legs together with butcher's twine.

Roast for 30 minutes, then reduce the heat to 350°F (177°C). Continue roasting for 30–45 minutes. Cooking time will depend on the size of the chicken. An instant-read thermometer should read at least 160°F (71°C) before you remove the chicken from the oven. Let the chicken rest 8–10 minutes before carving.

Serve with your favorite side dishes.

ACTIVE PREP: 20 minutes
TOTAL TIME: 35 minutes
SERVES: 2–4

Lamb

2 racks of lamb, frenched
2 Tbs fresh rosemary, chopped
2 Tbs garlic, minced
Kosher salt
Black pepper
Sprigs of fresh rosemary for garnish

White Beans

1 can white beans, great northern beans, or cannellini beans, drained and rinsed
1 cup (8 fl oz/237 ml) water
1 large shallot, sliced
2 Tbs garlic, minced
1 tsp fresh thyme, minced
Kosher salt
Black pepper

Peach Preserves

2 cup frozen peaches
1 cup (8 fl oz/237 ml) smoked porter
2 Tbs brown sugar

Alaskan Smoked Porter
(JUNEAU, AK)
Founders Smoked Porter
(GRAND RAPIDS, MI)
Captain Lawrence Smoked Porter
(ELMSFORD, NY)

Rack of Lamb with White Beans and Smoked Porter Peach Preserves

A frenched rack of lamb has the meat, fat, and membranes that connect the individual ribs removed. It gives the rack a clean look. You can do it yourself or ask your butcher to do it for you.

LAMB

Preheat the oven to 400°F (204°C). Rub the lamb with the rosemary and garlic and salt and pepper to taste. Place the lamb racks in a roasting pan and roast for 17–20 minutes. Add 7–10 minutes if you prefer a more well-done lamb. Let the racks rest 3–4 minutes before carving.

WHITE BEANS

In a small saucepan, combine the beans, water, shallot, garlic, and thyme. Bring to a boil. Reduce the heat and simmer for 10–12 minutes. Season to taste with salt and pepper.

PEACH PRESERVES

In a medium saucepan over medium heat, combine the ingredients, bring to a simmer, and cook down to a syrup consistency. If desired, puree the mixture.

For a dramatic presentation, cut each rack of lamb in half and interweave the rib bones. Spoon the white beans in a line across each plate. Arrange the lamb over the beans. Place a spoonful of the Smoked Porter Peach Preserves in front of each half-rack of lamb. Garnish with rosemary.

ACTIVE PREP: 15 minutes
TOTAL TIME: 25 minutes
SERVES: 2–4

Duck Breast

2 cup (16 fl oz/473 ml) root beer
4 cloves garlic
4 sprigs fresh thyme
2–4 duck breasts
Kosher salt
Black pepper

Wilted Greens

1 large bunch of kale, collards, or other greens
1 cup (8 fl oz/237 ml) chicken stock
Kosher salt
Black pepper

Oskar Blues B Stiff & Sons Root Beer
(LONGMONT, CO)
Virgil's Root Beer
(LOS ANGELES, CA)
Boylan's Root Beer
(MOONACHIE, NJ)

Root Beer– Marinated Duck Breast with Wilted Greens

DUCK BREAST

In a large shallow baking dish, combine the root beer, garlic, and thyme. Add the duck breasts. Cover and marinate in the refrigerator for up to 12 hours.

Remove the duck breasts from the marinade and pat the skin side dry with paper towels. Heat a large sauté pan over medium heat. Season the duck breasts with salt and pepper. Lay the breasts skin side down in the hot pan. Sear for 7–8 minutes until the skin becomes crisp and golden brown. Turn the duck over and continue to cook for another 7–8 minutes for medium-rare, longer if you prefer a more well-done duck. Remove the duck breasts from the pan and let rest for 2–3 minutes before slicing. Add the marinade to the pan, bring to a boil, and reduce to a syrup, then strain and keep warm until ready to serve.

WILTED GREENS

In a deep pan, combine the greens and chicken stock. Bring to a boil. Cover and reduce heat. Simmer for 15–20 minutes until the greens are completely tender. Season to taste with salt and pepper.

Arrange the greens on each plate. Slice the duck breasts into ¼-inch (6-mm) slices and arrange around the greens. Spoon the reduced root beer marinade over the sliced duck breasts.

ACTIVE PREP: 15 minutes
TOTAL TIME: 30 minutes
SERVES: 2–4

Pork

2 Tbs chili powder
2 Tbs smoked paprika
1 tsp garlic powder
1 tsp onion powder
1 tsp cumin
1 tsp cinnamon
1 Tbs kosher salt
1 Tbs black pepper
1 pork tenderloin, cleaned and trimmed

Mole Sauce

1½ cup (12 fl oz/355 ml) coffee stout
½ cup (4 fl oz/118 ml) tomato paste
1 Tbs peanut butter
1 Tbs cocoa powder
1 tsp chipotle powder
2 Tbs chili powder
2 Tbs garlic, minced
2 Tbs (1 fl oz/30 ml) molasses
Kosher salt
Black pepper

Alesmith Speedway Stout
(SAN DIEGO, CA)
Brewfist Spaghetti Western
(CODOGNO, ITALY)
Dieu du Ciel Péché Mortel
(MONTREAL, QUEBEC)

Chili-Dusted Pork Tenderloin with Coffee Stout Mole Sauce

PORK

Combine all the spices to make a rub. Coat the tenderloin generously with the rub. Let sit for 10–30 minutes in the refrigerator.

Preheat the oven to 450°F (232°C). Place the tenderloin on a rack in a roasting pan. Roast for 12 minutes. Turn off the oven after 12 minutes and leave the tenderloin for an additional 10–12 minutes. Remove the tenderloin from the oven and let it rest for 2–3 minutes before slicing.

MOLE SAUCE

In a small saucepan, combine the beer, tomato paste, peanut butter, cocoa powder, chipotle powder, chili powder, garlic, and molasses. Bring to a boil, whisking occasionally. Reduce the heat to a simmer and simmer for 8–10 minutes or until thickened to barbeque-sauce–like consistency. Season to taste with salt and pepper.

After the pork has rested, slice it into ½-inch (12-mm) to 1-inch (25-mm) slices. Top the slices with the Coffee Stout Mole Sauce or serve the sauce on the side.

ACTIVE PREP: 15 minutes
TOTAL TIME: 3–4 hours
SERVES: 2

Short Ribs

2 lb (907 g) beef short ribs
2 cup flour
Kosher salt
Black pepper
Olive oil
3 cup (24 fl oz/710 ml) Irish stout
1 large onion
1 large carrot
2 stalks celery
2–4 sprigs fresh thyme
4 cloves garlic
Beef stock or water

Mashed Potatoes

1 large russet potato
Kosher salt
¼ cup (2 fl oz/237 ml) whole milk
2 Tbs unsalted butter
1 Tbs (½ fl oz/15 ml) prepared horseradish
Black pepper

Alaskan Stout
(JUNEAU, AK)
Anderson Valley Barney Flats Stout
(BOONVILLE, CA)
Moylan's Dragoons
(NOVATO, CA)

Irish Stout–Braised Short Ribs with Horseradish Mashed Potatoes

STOUT-BRAISED SHORT RIBS

Preheat the oven to 300°F (149°C).

Season the short ribs with salt and pepper. Dredge the ribs in flour. In a deep sauté pan with a lid, heat 2 tablespoons (1 fl oz/30 ml) of olive oil. Carefully place the short ribs in the hot oil. Sear 3–4 minutes on each side until the meat begins to brown. Add the beer, onion, carrot, celery, thyme, and garlic. Add the beef stock or water to bring the liquid level up to the top of the short ribs. Bring to a boil.

Cover the pan and place the covered pan in the preheated oven. Cook for 2–3 hours, until the meat is fork tender.

Remove the short ribs from the liquid. Strain the sauce, season it with salt and pepper, and serve with the short ribs.

HORSERADISH MASHED POTATOES

Peel and quarter the potato. Place in a small saucepan with 1 teaspoon of salt and cover with water. Bring the potato and water to a boil and boil until tender. Drain the water. Add the milk, butter, and horseradish. Mash to desired consistency. Season to taste with salt and pepper.

ACTIVE PREP: 25 minutes
TOTAL TIME: 45 minutes
SERVES: 4–8

Pork Loin

2 cup walnut halves or pieces
4 Tbs fresh sage
2 cloves of garlic
2 Tbs (1 fl oz/30 ml) extra-virgin olive oil
1 pork loin
Kosher salt
Black pepper

Apple Chutney

4 green apples, peeled, cored, and diced
4 Tbs (½ stick) unsalted butter
1½ cup (12 fl oz/355 ml) hard cider
Pinch of salt

Angry Orchard Muse
(CINCINNATI, OH)
Moa Apple
(BLENHEIM, NEW ZEALAND)
Foggy Ridge First Fruit
(DUGSPUR, VA)

Sage-and-Walnut-Crusted Pork Loin with Hard Cider Apple Chutney

This is a great fall dish that pairs well with sides such as butternut squash, sweet potatoes, or even roasted turnips.

PORK LOIN

Heat a dry sauté pan over medium heat. Add the walnut pieces and toast lightly. In the bowl of a food processor, combine the toasted walnuts, sage, garlic, and olive oil. Pulse 3 times for 3 seconds each time.

Preheat the oven to 350°F (177°C). Season the pork loin with salt and pepper. Generously coat the pork loin with the walnut crust, being sure to really press the coating into the meat.

Place the pork loin on a rack in a roasting pan and roast for 35–40 minutes. An instant-read thermometer should read 145°F (63°C) before you remove the pork loin from the oven. Let the pork loin rest for 8–10 minutes before carving.

APPLE CHUTNEY

In a large heavy-bottom skillet over medium-high heat, cook the apples in the butter until the apples begin to caramelize. Add the hard cider and salt and continue cooking until the liquid has reduced to a glaze.

To serve, slice the pork loin and top with the Hard Cider Apple Chutney.

ACTIVE PREP: 30 minutes
TOTAL TIME: 45 minutes
SERVES: 2

Beef

1 Tbs (½ fl oz/15 ml) extra-virgin olive oil
1 tsp fresh rosemary, finely chopped
1 shallot, minced
Kosher salt
Black pepper
1 lb (454 g) beef tenderloin or 2 filets mignons

Carrots and Shallots

1 bunch of baby carrots, scrubbed and tops trimmed
3 shallots, peeled and halved lengthwise
1 Tbs fresh thyme, chopped
2 Tbs unsalted butter, melted
Kosher salt
Black pepper

Rauchbier Au Jus

1 shallot, minced
1 bay leaf
½ cup (4 fl oz/118 ml) Rauchbier
2 cup (16 fl oz/473 ml) beef broth
Kosher salt

Jack's Abby Smoke & Dagger
(FRAMINGHAM, MA)
Fort Collins Brewery Z Lager
(FORT COLLINS, CO)
Ballast Point Abandon Ship Smoked Lager
(SAN DIEGO, CA)

Beef Tenderloin with Roasted Carrots and Shallots and Rauchbier Au Jus

BEEF

In a small dish, combine the olive oil, rosemary, shallot, and salt and pepper to taste. Coat the beef tenderloin or filets mignons with the rub. Marinate at room temperature for 15–20 minutes before cooking. Grill, or roast in a preheated 400°F (204°C) oven, depending on which you prefer, to your desired temperature (medium-rare is 130°F/54°C to 135°F/57°C). Remember that the meat will continue cooking after it is removed from the grill or oven, so leave room for this carry-over cooking.

ROASTED CARROTS AND SHALLOTS

Preheat the oven to 400°F (204°C). In a small roasting pan, toss together the carrots, shallots, thyme, butter, and salt and pepper to taste, coating the vegetables well with the melted butter. Roast for 10–12 minutes, until tender and lightly browned.

RAUCHBIER AU JUS

In a small saucepan, combine all the ingredients and bring to a boil. Continue boiling until reduced by about 50 percent. Season to taste with salt.

Let the meat rest for a couple of minutes before carving (the tenderloin). Serve with the roasted carrots and shallots. Pour Rauchbier Au Jus over the meat or serve on the side.

ACTIVE PREP: 35 minutes
TOTAL TIME: 60 minutes
SERVES: 4

Schnitzel

1 cup all-purpose flour
3 eggs, beaten
2 cup bread crumbs
4 cutlets of veal, chicken, pork, or turkey
Kosher salt
Black pepper
Canola oil
Zest from 1 lemon

Potatoes

2 slices bacon, diced
1 small red onion, thinly sliced
2 cloves of garlic
1 lb (454 g) red skin or fingerling potatoes, sliced
1 Tbs (½ fl oz/15 ml) whole-grain mustard
1 cup (8 fl oz/237 ml) German beer
1 Tbs (½ fl oz/15 ml) apple cider vinegar
1 Tbs fresh parsley, chopped
Kosher salt
Black Pepper

Pickled Red Cabbage

1 head of red cabbage, cored and sliced
1 cup (8 fl oz/237 ml) apple cider vinegar
½ cup sugar
Kosher salt
Black pepper

Works with just about any German or German-style beer, from pilsner and helles to dopplebock.

Schnitzel with German-Style Potatoes and Pickled Red Cabbage

SCHNITZEL

You will need 3 bowls for your breading station. Place the flour in the first bowl, the beaten eggs in the second bowl, and combine the bread crumbs and lemon zest in the third bowl. Season the cutlets with salt and pepper. Dredge them in the flour, dip them in the egg wash, and coat them with bread crumbs. After all the cutlets are breaded, heat 3–4 tablespoons of canola oil in a large skillet on medium-high heat. Pan-fry the cutlets for 3–4 minutes per side. Wipe out the skillet with paper towels between batches if needed.

POTATOES

In a large sauté pan with a lid, cook the bacon until crisp and all the fat has been rendered. Remove the bacon from the pan with a slotted spoon. In the bacon drippings, sauté the onions and garlic until tender. Add the sliced potatoes and cook for 6–8 minutes stirring often. Stir in the mustard, beer, vinegar, and parsley and cover the pan. Cook for 7–10 minutes. Remove the lid and continue cooking until the potatoes are fully cooked and the sauce has thickened slightly. Fold the bacon into the potatoes. Season to taste with salt and pepper.

PICKLED RED CABBAGE

In a large nonreactive saucepan, combine the cabbage, vinegar, sugar, and salt and pepper to taste. Cover and bring to a boil. Cook until the cabbage is tender. Remove the lid and cook until the liquid has almost completely evaporated.

Top the schnitzel with the Pickled Red Cabbage and serve with the German-style Potatoes.

¼ cup (2 fl oz/59 ml) canola oil
4–6 rabbit hind legs (substitute chicken legs if you prefer)
Kosher salt
Black pepper
1 cup all-purpose flour
1 large onion, diced
1 can San Marzano tomatoes
1 cup button mushrooms, sliced
1 red bell pepper, diced
1 cup (8 fl oz/237 ml) Italian lager or other pilsner style
1 tsp fresh rosemary, chopped
1 tsp fresh sage, chopped,
1 Tbs fresh parsley, chopped

Victory Brewing Prima Pils
(DOWNINGTOWN, PA)
New Belgium Blue Paddle
(FORT COLLINS, CO)
Firestone Walker Pivo Hoppy Pils
(PASO ROBLES, CA)

Slow Cooker Rabbit Cacciatore

We had some wonderful local organic chicken available when we prepared this dish for the photo shoot, so we substituted chicken for the rabbit.

In a skillet over medium-high heat, heat the canola oil. Season the rabbit with salt and pepper. Dredge the rabbit in the flour and shake to remove excess. Brown the rabbit in the skillet and place the browned pieces in a slow cooker. Combine the remaining ingredients and pour over the rabbit pieces. Cover the slow cooker and cook 4–6 hours on high or 6–8 hours on low. Season to taste with salt and pepper.

Serve rabbit cacciatore over pasta, rice, polenta, potatoes, or other grain.

ACTIVE PREP: 30 minutes
TOTAL TIME: 8 hours
SERVES: 4

Confit

½ cup brown sugar
1½ cup (12 fl oz/355 ml) ESB
2 lb (907 g) chicken thighs, rinsed and dried
2 Tbs (1 fl oz/30 ml) + 2 cup (16 fl oz/
473 ml) canola or vegetable oil
2 shallots
4 cloves garlic
2 sprigs fresh thyme
16 Tbs (2 sticks) unsalted butter, melted
Kosher salt
Black pepper

Ratatouille

1 red onion, diced
4 cloves garlic, minced
2 Tbs (1 fl oz/30 ml) extra-virgin olive oil
1 medium eggplant, peeled and diced
1 zucchini, diced
1 yellow squash, diced
1 ripe tomato, diced
1 Tbs fresh thyme, chopped
Kosher salt
Black pepper

1 jar preserved lemons
Fresh parsley or micro-greens

Fuller's ESB
(CHISWICK, ENGLAND)
AleSmith Anvil Ale ESB
(SAN DIEGO, CA)
Left Hand Sawtooth Ale
(LONGMONT, CO)

Confit of Chicken with Ratatouille

CONFIT

Dissolve the brown sugar into the ESB. Place the chicken thighs in a large resealable zipper bag or other sealable container. Pour in the beer/sugar mixture and marinate for at least 4 hours and up to 24 hours.

Preheat the oven to 300°F (149°C). Remove the thighs from the marinade and let them drain in a colander while you begin heating 2 tablespoons oil in a large sauté pan. Sear the thighs until well browned on both sides. Place in a baking dish, add the shallots, garlic, and thyme, then pour in the melted butter and 2 cups of oil until just covered. Season to taste with salt and pepper. Cover the pan with a lid or foil and bake for 3 hours. Carefully remove the thighs from the hot oil/butter using a slotted spoon. Let the thighs cool on a cooling rack set over a sheet pan to allow excess oil to drain off. When ready to serve, heat a skillet over medium-high heat and sear each piece until crispy and golden brown.

RATATOUILLE

In a large pot, sweat the onion and garlic with the olive oil. After 3–4 minutes, add the eggplant and cook for 5–6 minutes. Add the zucchini, yellow squash, tomato, and thyme and cover the pot. Continue cooking for 8–10 minutes, stirring occasionally. Season to taste with salt and pepper. The ratatouille should resemble a thick vegetable stew.

To serve, place a large spoonful of ratatouille in the center of each plate. Top the ratatouille with a chicken thigh confit. Garnish with thinly sliced preserved lemon and fresh parsley or micro-greens.

PASTA, RICE, AND DUMPLINGS

ACTIVE PREP: 50 minutes
TOTAL TIME: 80 minutes
SERVES: 4

Wheat-Beer Pasta Dough

3 cup all-purpose flour
½ tsp kosher salt
2 large eggs
½ cup (4 fl oz/118 ml) wheat beer

Orecchiette

½ batch wheat-beer pasta dough
2 Tbs (1 fl oz/30 ml) extra-virgin olive oil
1 lb (454 g) fresh Italian sausage
2 cup small broccoli florets
2 Tbs minced garlic
1 cup freshly grated Parmesan

3 Floyds Gumballhead
(MUNSTER, IN)
Bell's Oberon
(KALAMAZOO, MI)
Boulevard 80-Acre Hoppy Wheat
(KANSAS CITY, MI)

Orecchiette with Italian Sausage and Broccoli

WHEAT-BEER PASTA DOUGH

In the bowl of a stand mixer with a hook attachment, combine the flour and salt until they're thoroughly mixed. Create an indentation in the dry mixture and add the beer and eggs. Mix for about 6 minutes on low speed to fully incorporate the beer and eggs. Remove the dough to a lightly floured surface and hand-knead for 10 minutes or until the consistency of the dough is elastic and free of any lumps or air bubbles. Place the dough in a mixing bowl, cover with a towel, and let the dough stand for 30 minutes. The dough may also be stored in the refrigerator for up to 48 hours.

ORECCHIETTE

To make the orecchiette, roll a portion of your pasta dough into a rope about ½-inch (13-mm) thick on a floured surface. Cut the rope into pieces about ½-inch (13-mm) long. Place one piece in the palm of your hand and using the thumb of your other hand flatten the dough into a disk shape no thicker than ⅛ inch (3 mm). Leave an indentation in the center of your pasta (this is what gives orecchiette its name, "little ears").

Bring a large pot of salted water to a boil. In a large sauté pan over medium heat, heat the olive oil. Add the sausage and cook until lightly browned, breaking it up as it cooks. Meanwhile, steam the broccoli for 3 minutes. Once the sausage is browned, cook the pasta. Drop the orecchiette into the boiling water and cook for 3–4 minutes. The pasta will float when fully cooked. Remove the cooked pasta with a slotted spoon and add it to the pan with the sausage. Add the broccoli and garlic and sauté for 2–3 minutes. Remove from the heat.

Serve in pasta bowls topped with the freshly grated Parmesan.

ACTIVE PREP: 45 minutes
TOTAL TIME: 60 minutes
SERVES: 4

Agnolotti Filling

1 butternut squash, peeled, halved, and seeded
1 large shallot
2 Tbs minced garlic
1 Tbs fresh thyme, chopped
1 tsp cinnamon
1 pinch of nutmeg
1 cup (8 fl oz/237 ml) Oktoberfest
2 Tbs unsalted butter
Kosher salt
Black pepper

Agnolotti

½ batch Wheat-Beer Pasta Dough (see page 108)
1 egg, beaten

Brown Butter Sauce

8 Tbs (1 stick) unsalted butter
6–8 fresh sage leaves
Zest of 1 orange
2 Tbs (1 fl oz/30 ml) Oktoberfest
Kosher salt

Great Lakes Oktoberfest
(CLEVELAND, OH)
Ayinger Oktober Fest-Marzen
(AYING, GERMANY)
Left Hand Oktoberfest
(LONGMONT, CO)

Butternut Squash Agnolotti with Oktoberfest Brown Butter Sauce

AGNOLOTTI FILLING

Dice the squash into 1-inch (25-mm) pieces. In a deep sauté pan with a lid, combine the squash, shallot, garlic, thyme, cinnamon, nutmeg, beer, and butter. Bring to a boil. Cover and reduce heat to medium. Cook for 10–12 minutes or until the squash is soft. Place the mixture in a food processor bowl and process until smooth. Season to taste with salt and pepper. Let cool completely before filling pasta.

AGNOLOTTI

Using a rolling pin or pasta machine, roll out the dough into thin sheets (the lowest setting on the pasta machine). Cut the pasta sheets into 24–36 inches (60–90 cm) pieces. Place one sheet on your work surface. Place 1 tablespoon of filling every 2 inches (5 cm) in rows 2 inches (5 cm) apart across the sheet, leaving a 1-inch (25-mm) border around the edges. Cover with another pasta sheet and press firmly between the fillings to seal each individual agnolotti. Use a pasta cutter or sharp knife to cut out the agnolotti. Repeat until you've used all the pasta sheets.

BROWN BUTTER SAUCE

Bring a large pot of salted water to a boil. In a heavy-bottom pan over medium-high heat, melt and heat the butter until it starts to darken, 6–8 minutes. Remove from the heat. Add the sage and orange zest. Let cool to room temperature, then add the beer. To serve, reheat the sauce over low heat just long enough for it to start to bubble. Season to taste with salt.

Cook the agnolotti in the salted boiling water until they float to the surface. Remove with a slotted spoon and place directly into the brown butter sauce. Heat for 1 minute.

ACTIVE PREP: 25 minutes
TOTAL TIME: 35 minutes
SERVES: 4

Spaetzle

3 eggs
1 pinch nutmeg
5 fl oz (148 ml) maibock
2 cup all-purpose flour
Kosher salt
Black pepper
Olive oil

1 bunch Swiss chard, washed and trimmed
4–6 oz (113–170 g) thick-cut bacon, cut into 1" (25-mm) pieces
4 eggs

Fort Collins Brewery Maibock
(FORT COLLINS, CO)
Hofbräu Maibock
(MÜNCHEN, GERMANY)
Boulevard Boss Tom's Golden Bock
(KANSAS CITY, MO)

German Beer Spaetzle with Sautéed Swiss Chard, Bacon, and Fried Egg

SPAETZLE

Mix the eggs, nutmeg, and beer until blended. Add flour until a thick batter-like consistency is achieved (a thick pancake batter is the best example).

Bring salted water to a boil in a large pot. Push the spaetzle through a spaetzle maker or colander into the boiling water and simmer for 1–2 minutes until the spaetzle float to the surface. Drain the spaetzle and spread out on a cookie sheet. Lightly oil and let cool while preparing the rest of dish.

In a large nonstick sauté pan, cook the bacon until the fat is almost completely rendered and the bacon is beginning to crisp. Tear the chard into small pieces and add directly to the bacon. Cover and cook for 2–3 minutes over medium heat stirring occasionally. Remove the lid and add the spaetzle to the pan. Increase the heat to medium-high and sauté until the spaetzle begins to brown lightly.

To serve, top with a fried egg cooked to each person's liking.

ACTIVE PREP: 40 minutes
TOTAL TIME: 60 minutes
SERVES: 2

Gnocchi

½ cup dehydrated potato flakes
¼ cup (2 fl oz/59 ml) pumpkin beer
1 cup pumpkin puree
1 egg
2 Tbs sugar
1 tsp nutmeg
1 tsp ground ginger
¾ cup all-purpose flour, plus more for rolling later
Kosher salt
Black pepper
2 Tbs unsalted butter

Reduction

1½ cup (12 fl oz/355 ml) pumpkin beer

Pepitas

1 tsp unsalted butter
2 Tbs pepitas
Pinch of cayenne
Kosher salt

Roasted Mushrooms

1 Tbs unsalted butter
4 large button mushrooms, stems removed

Lakefront Pumpkin Lager
(MILWAUKEE, WI)
Alewerks Pumpkin Ale
(WILLIAMSBURG, VA)
Anderson Valley Fall Hornin' Pumpkin Ale
(BOONVILLE, CA)

Gnocchi with Pumpkin Beer Reduction and Roasted Mushrooms

GNOCCHI

In a large bowl, combine the potato flakes and beer. Add the pumpkin, egg, sugar, and spices. Mix well. Slowly incorporate the flour until a thick, mostly dry, dough forms. Turn the dough out onto a floured surface. Dust with flour and knead gently for 3–4 minutes, adding a little flour as necessary, until the dough is slightly elastic and smooth. Divide the dough into 4 portions. Roll each portion out into a rope ¾-inch (19-mm) thick. Cut the rope into 1-inch (25-mm) pieces. Reserve.

REDUCTION

In a small saucepan, bring the beer to a boil. Reduce the heat to a simmer and cook until the beer is reduced to a syrup.

PEPITAS

In a small saucepan over low heat, melt the butter, then add the cayenne and pepitas. Slowly toast the pepitas for 3 minutes. Season lightly with salt.

ROASTED MUSHROOMS

Preheat the oven to 400°F (204°C). In a small pan over medium-high heat, melt the butter. Place the mushrooms top down in the butter and cook for 2 minutes. Turn over and finsh in the oven for 5 minutes.

Drop the gnocchi pieces into a pot of boiling salted water and cook for 3–4 minutes, until the gnocchi float to the surface. Remove the gnocchi and drain. In a large sauté pan over medium-high heat, melt 2 tablespoons of butter. Add the gnocchi and sauté until lightly browned. Add a little of the beer reduction and toss to coat the gnocchi. Remove from the heat. Add the pepitas and stir gently.

Divide the gnocchi between 2 pasta bowls. Top with the Roasted Mushrooms, whole or sliced, and drizzle more of the Pumpkin Beer Reduction over the top.

ACTIVE PREP: 35 minutes
TOTAL TIME: 45 minutes
SERVES: 4

Pierogi Dough

2 cup all-purpose flour, plus extra for kneading and rolling the dough
½ tsp kosher salt
1 large egg, beaten
½ cup sour cream, plus extra to serve with the pierogi
4 Tbs (½ stick) unsalted butter, softened and cut into small pieces

Pierogi Filling

1 medium sweet potato, peeled and diced
1 cup dried apricots
1½ cup (12 fl oz/355 ml) apricot ale
Kosher salt
Black pepper

Caramelized Onions

1 large onion, peeled and thinly sliced
4 Tbs (½ stick) unsalted butter, divided
Pinch of kosher salt

¼ cup roasted, salted peanuts
Aged balsamic vinegar, the older the better

Samuel Smith's Organic Apricot Ale
(TADCASTER, ENGLAND)
Dry Dock Apricot Blonde
(AURORA, CO)

Sweet Potato & Apricot Pierogies with Caramelized Onions

PIEROGI DOUGH
Combine all the ingredients in a large bowl and mix until a soft dough forms. If the dough is sticky, add just a little bit of flour and mix some more. Wrap the dough in plastic wrap and refrigerate for at least 1 hour.

PIEROGI FILLING
Place the sweet potato, apricots, and beer in a pot. Add just enough water to cover the ingredients by 1-inch (25 mm). Bring to a boil and cook until the sweet potato is fully cooked and tender. Drain the liquid. In a food processor, puree the sweet potato and apricots until smooth. Season to taste with salt and pepper. Let cool before filling the pierogies.

Place the chilled dough on a floured work surface and roll out to about 1/16-inch (16-mm) thick. Cut out 3-inch (7.6-cm) circles. Place a spoonful of filling slightly off-center of each dough circle. Fold the dough over the filling to form half moons and pinch to seal the seam closed. Cover and refrigerate.

CARAMELIZED ONIONS
In a wide, thick-bottomed sauté pan over medium-high heat, melt 2 tablespoons of butter until wisps of smoke form. Add the onion slices and stir to coat the onions. Spread the onions out evenly in the pan, reduce the heat to medium, and let the onions cook, stirring every few minutes, until they begin to take on a peanut-butter color, 10–15 minutes. Season with salt.

Gently drop the pierogies into a large pot of boiling salted water. Cook for 3–4 minutes. While pierogies cook, melt 2 tablespoons of butter in a large sauté pan over medium heat. Once the pierogies are cooked, remove them from the water and place them in the sauté pan with the butter. Let the pierogies crisp and brown on one side, then flip to do the same. Add the caramelized onion and gently mix. Remove from the heat.

Arrange the pierogies and caramelized onions on plates. Sprinkle with the salted peanuts and drizzle with the balsamic vinegar.

ACTIVE PREP: 55 minutes
TOTAL TIME: 55 minutes
SERVES: 4

½ cup pancetta or thick-sliced bacon, diced
2 cup Arborio rice
1 shallot, minced
1½ cup (12 fl oz/355 ml) saison
2–3 qt (1.9–2.8 l) water or stock
1 cup white cheddar, shredded
1 Tbs fresh rosemary or thyme, chopped
1 cup asparagus tips, blanched in salted water
Kosher salt
Black pepper

Brasserie DuPont Saison
(TOURPES, BELGIUM)
Firestone Walker Opal
(PASO ROBLES, CA)
Boulevard Tank 7
(KANSAS CITY, MO)
Brasserie Fantôme Saison
(SOY, BELGIUM)

Risotto with White Cheddar, Pancetta, and Asparagus

In a deep sauté pan, cook the pancetta over medium-high heat until crisp and browned. Remove the cooked pancetta from the pan using a slotted spoon. Turn the heat to low and add the Arborio rice and shallot to the pan with the pancetta drippings. Stir well and toast the rice for about 2 minutes. Deglaze the pan with the beer. Cook until the rice almost completely absorbs the beer. Add just enough water or stock to cover the rice. Reduce the heat to medium and continue cooking, stirring constantly, until the liquid is almost completely absorbed once again. Repeat the process of adding liquid and cooking until the rice is fully cooked. Be sure to stir slowly and frequently. This process can take 30–45 minutes before the rice is tender. Once the risotto is fully cooked, remove from the heat. Fold in the cheese and herbs. Season to taste with salt and pepper. Fold in the warm blanched asparagus tips just before serving.

DESSERTS

ACTIVE PREP: 15 minutes
TOTAL TIME: 50 minutes
SERVES: 4

Cherry Filling

Nonstick cooking spray
3 cup pitted cherries or berries (frozen work well)
½ cup (4 fl oz/118 ml) Kriek lambic
2 Tbs all-purpose flour
½ cup white sugar

Topping

½ cup quick-cooking oats
½ cup all-purpose flour
½ cup packed brown sugar
6 Tbs (¾ stick) unsalted butter, melted

Brasserie Cantillon Kriek Lambic
(BRUSSELS, BELGIUM)
New Belgium Transatlantique Kriek
(FORT COLLINS, CO)
Lindeman's Kriek Lambic
(VLEZENBEEK, BELGIUM)
Drie Fonteinen Oude Kriek
(BEERSEL, BELGIUM)

Cherry Berry Lambic Crisp

Preheat the oven to 325°F (163°C). Spray four 6-ounce (177-ml) ramekins with nonstick cooking spray. In a medium saucepan mix the cherries, Kriek, 2 tablespoons flour, and white sugar. Bring to a boil and immediately remove from the heat. Evenly distribute the cherry mixture among the 4 prepared rame-kins. Combine the quick-cooking oats, remaining flour, brown sugar, and melted butter. Crumble the mixture evenly over the cherry mixture. Bake for 30–35 minutes or until golden brown and bubbling. Let cool slightly, then serve alone or with vanilla-bean ice cream.

ACTIVE PREP: 25 minutes
TOTAL TIME: 60 minutes
SERVES: 2–4

Pears

1½–3 cup (12–24 fl oz/355–710 ml) lager
½ cup (4 fl oz/118 ml) honey
Rind of one orange, left in peels (not zested)
1 cinnamon stick (optional)
1 vanilla bean pod, split lengthwise
2–4 slightly under-ripe pears (one per person)

Sabayon

6 egg yolks
½ cup sugar
¼ cup (2 fl oz/59 ml) poaching liquid from the pears, cooled and strained

New Belgium Summer Helles
(FORT COLLINS, CO)
Sierra Nevada Summerfest
(CHICO, CA)
Victory Lager
(DOWNINGTOWN, PA)

Summerfest Poached Pears with Sabayon

PEARS

In a small saucepan, combine the beer, honey, orange peel, cinnamon, and vanilla beans. Heat the mixture over medium heat until it begins to simmer.

While the poaching liquid is heating, peel the pears with a vegetable peeler. As you finish peeling the pears, place them directly into the poaching liquid. Once all the pears are in the poaching liquid, cover the pot and simmer for 15–20 minutes or until the pears are tender. You should be able to pierce them easily with a sharp knife.

Remove the pears from the liquid and cool completely before serving. You can prepare the poached pears up to 24 hours in advance.

SABAYON

Combine all the ingredients in a stainless steel or glass bowl or a double-boiler insert. Place the bowl over a pot of simmering water and whisk constantly until the mixture is thick and foamy (like whipped cream).

To serve, you can either slice the pear or leave it whole; both are nice presentations. Place each pear on a plate. Spoon the sabayon around the pear.

ACTIVE PREP: 35 minutes
TOTAL TIME: 75 minutes
SERVES: 6–8

Profiteroles

1 cup (8 fl oz/237 ml) pumpkin ale
4 Tbs (½ stick) unsalted butter
¼ teaspoon kosher salt
1 cup all-purpose flour
3 large eggs
2 Tbs brown sugar

Mousse

1 cup (8 fl oz/237 ml) heavy cream
1 cup granulated sugar
1 cup mascarpone
2 Tbs (1 fl oz/30 ml) pure maple syrup
1 Tbs (½ fl oz/15 ml) vanilla
1 tsp grated nutmeg
1 tsp ginger powder
Powdered sugar (optional)

Alewerks Pumpkin Ale
(WILLIAMSBURG, VA)
Anderson Valley Fall Hornin' Pumpkin Ale
(BOONVILLE, CA)

Pumpkin Ale Profiteroles with Maple Mascarpone Mousse

PROFITEROLES

Preheat the oven to 400°F (204°C). Line 2 cookie sheets with parchment paper. In a medium saucepan over medium-high heat, bring the beer, butter, and salt just to a boil. Turn off the heat, add all the flour, and stir vigorously with a wooden spoon until a dough forms. Turn the heat back on to medium and continue mixing until the dough dries out, pulls away from the sides of the pan, and forms a smooth ball, 1–2 minutes. Transfer the dough to the bowl of a food processor and let it cool it for 5–6 minutes so it won't cook the eggs when you add them. Process for 5 seconds.

Add the eggs and brown sugar to the processor bowl and process until the eggs are well mixed in, 10–15 seconds. The dough should appear smooth and shiny. Transfer the dough to a bowl and let it cool for 10 minutes.

Scoop tablespoon-size mounds onto the parchment-covered sheet, spacing about 2 inches (5 cm) apart. Bake for 15 minutes. Reduce the heat to 350°F (177°C) and continue baking until golden brown and crisp, about 15 minutes. Cool completely.

MOUSSE

Combine the cream and sugar in the bowl of a mixer fitted with a wire whip attachment. Begin whisking on low speed. Gradually increase the speed to high. Beat for 2–3 minutes, until the cream is firm and fluffy. Add the mascarpone, maple syrup, vanilla, and spices. Beat another 30 seconds. Refrigerate 1 hour.

Cut a slice from the top of each profiterole, fill the profiterole with mousse, and replace the top. Dust with powdered sugar if desired.

ACTIVE PREP: 15 minutes
TOTAL TIME: 2 hours
SERVES: 8

Cake

8 Tbs (1 stick) unsalted butter, softened
1¾ cup white sugar
2 eggs
1 cup (8 fl oz/237 ml) applesauce
½ cup (4 fl oz/118 ml) winter ale
2½ cup all-purpose flour
1½ tsp baking soda
½ tsp baking powder
1 Tbs ground cinnamon
1 tsp nutmeg
1 tsp ginger
½ tsp clove
Pinch of kosher salt

Glaze

1 cup toasted coconut
Zest and juice of 1 orange
1 Tbs (½ fl oz/15 ml) vanilla
3 cup powdered sugar
12 Tbs (1½ sticks) unsalted butter, melted
1 Tbs lemon juice

Bell's Winter White Ale
(KALAMAZOO, MI)
Weyerbacher Winter Ale
(EASTON, PA)
Alaskan Winter Ale
(JUNEAU, AK)
Summit Winter Ale
(ST. PAUL, MN)

Winter Ale Spice Cake with Toasted Orange Coconut Glaze

CAKE

Preheat the oven to 350°F (177°C). Grease and flour a bundt cake pan.

In the bowl of a mixer, cream the butter and sugar on medium speed for 2 minutes. Add the eggs one at a time being sure not to add the second egg until the first egg is fully incorporated. Add the applesauce and beer. Mix for another minute.

In a separate bowl, combine the dry ingredients, then add the dry ingredients to the batter. Mix on low speed until just combined. Pour the cake batter into the prepared cake pan. Bake for 45–60 minutes, or until a toothpick inserted in the center comes out clean. Cool completely before glazing.

GLAZE

In a medium bowl, mix the ingredients until well combined. Pour over the cooled cake.

1 cup (8 fl oz/237 ml) milk stout
1 cup granulated sugar
12 oz (340 g) premium semisweet or
bittersweet chocolate, finely chopped
4 Tbs (½ stick) unsalted butter, room
temperature
6 large eggs
2 Tbs all-purpose flour
1 Tbs (½ fl oz/15 ml) pure vanilla extract
1 cup (8 fl oz/237 ml) whipping cream,
whipped

Left Hand Milk Stout
(LONGMONT, CO)
Firestone Walker Velvet Merkin
(PASO ROBLES, CA)

Chocolate Milk Stout Torte

Preheat the oven to 350°F (177°C).

In a large saucepan over medium-high heat, bring the beer and sugar to a boil. Remove from the heat and add the chocolate and butter. Stir slowly until the chocolate has completely melted and everything is incorporated. You should have a thick hot fudge-like consistency.

Mix in the eggs, one at a time. Add the flour and vanilla.

Grease a 9-inch (23-cm) cake pan or springform pan and line the bottom with parchment paper. Pour the batter into the prepared pan and shake or tap lightly to remove any air bubbles. Bake for 45–60 minutes. Rotate about halfway through if the oven heat is uneven. The cake will rise some but should collapse as it cools, leaving you a dense, moist, and decadent dessert. Cool for at least 1 hour before serving.

I like to serve this simply with fresh whipped cream, but you could you use this torte as a base for mousses and ganaches as well.

ACTIVE PREP: 20 minutes
TOTAL TIME: 45 minutes
SERVES: 6–8

Pudding

8 Tbs (1 stick) unsalted butter, room temperature, plus more for the pan

1 cup sugar

¼ cup (2 fl oz/59 ml) molasses

2 large eggs

1 Tbs (½ fl oz/15 ml) pure vanilla extract

1½ cup all-purpose flour, plus more for the pan

2 tsp baking powder

1 tsp cinnamon

Pinch of nutmeg

Pinch of kosher salt

8 oz (227 g) pitted dates, finely chopped and soaked in warm water to reconstitute

Caram-Ale Sauce

1 cup (packed) light brown sugar

1 cup (8 fl oz/237 ml) English-style cream ale

¼ cup (2 fl oz/59 ml) heavy cream

4 Tbs (½ stick) unsalted butter

1 tsp vanilla extract

Sixpoint Sweet Action
(BROOKLYN, NY)
New Glarus Spotted Cow
(NEW GLARUS, WI)
Anderson Valley Summer Solstice
(BOONVILLE, CA)

Sticky Toffee Pudding with Caram-Ale Sauce

PUDDING

Preheat the oven to 350°F (177°C). Butter and flour a 9-inch (23-cm) cake pan or individual ramekins.

In the bowl of an electric mixer, cream the butter and sugar. Add the molasses and mix well. Add the eggs, one at a time, beating well after each egg. Add the vanilla. Sift together the dry ingredients and add to the wet mixture in 2 batches. Mix until just combined. Add the dates and mix again for just a few seconds.

Pour the cake batter into the prepared cake pan or individual ramekins. Bake for 35–45 minutes, until set and a toothpick inserted in the center comes out clean.

CARAM-ALE SAUCE

In a small saucepan, combine all the ingredients and bring them to a boil. Reduce the heat and boil for 3–5 minutes, until slightly thickened. The sauce will thicken as it cools.

The Sticky Toffee Pudding is best served warm with Caram-Ale sauce over the top. Serve with ice cream or fresh whipped cream if desired.

ACTIVE PREP: 15 minutes
TOTAL TIME: 1 hour
SERVES: 6–8

1 cup (8 fl oz/237 ml) malt extract syrup
5 whole eggs
¾ cup sugar
1 cup (8 fl oz/237 ml) pale ale
1 tsp vanilla extract
Pinch of kosher salt
2 cup (16 fl oz/473 ml) heavy cream

3 Floyds Yum Yum
(MUNSTER, IN)
Drake's 1500
(SAN LEANDRO, CA)
Lagunitas New DogTown Pale Ale
(LAGUINTAS, CA)

Malt Syrup Crème Caramel

Preheat the oven to 325°F (163°C). Place 6–8 ramekins in a roasting pan. Evenly distribute the malt extract syrup among the ramekins.

Combine the eggs, sugar, beer, vanilla, and salt in a bowl. In a small saucepan, bring the heavy cream to a boil, then immediately remove from the heat. Slowly whisk the hot cream into the egg mixture. Pour this custard into the ramekins. Fill the roasting pan with 1 inch (25 mm) of hot water. Carefully place the roasting pan in the oven and bake for 45–60 minutes. The custard should be firm in the center when fully cooked. Carefully remove the pan from the oven and remove the ramekins from the pan. Let the custard cool for 20–30 minutes. Refrigerate for 1 hour before serving.

To serve, place the ramekins in a shallow pan of hot water for about 5 minutes just to soften the syrup. Run a knife around the outer edge of the ramekin. Invert onto a plate and slowly lift the ramekin. The malt extract syrup should pour over the custard.

ACTIVE PREP: 15 minutes
TOTAL TIME: 2 hours
SERVES: 4–8

Panna Cotta

1 package powdered gelatin
2 Tbs (1 fl oz/30 ml) water
½ cup (4 fl oz/118 ml) honey beer or mead
¼ cup (2 fl oz/59 ml) honey
1½ cup (12 fl oz/355 ml) Greek yogurt

Preserves

2 cup fresh or frozen peaches, peeled and sliced
½ cup sugar
1 Tbs (½ fl oz/15 ml) fresh lemon juice
¼ cup (2 fl oz/59 ml) orange juice
1 tsp fruit pectin

Honey

Kuhnhenn Orange Blossom Mead
(WARREN, MI)
Moonlight Meadery Sensual Mead
(LONDONDERRY, NH)
Casey Brewing & Blending East Bank
Honey Saison
(GLENWOOD SPRINGS, CO)
Hill Farmstead Anna Honey Saison
(GREENSBORO BEND, VT)

Honey Beer Panna Cotta with Peach Preserves and Honey

PANNA COTTA

In a small dish, combine the gelatin and water. Let sit for 5 minutes. In a small saucepan, bring the beer and honey to a boil and remove from the heat. Stir in the gelatin until it is completely dissolved. Slowly whisk in the yogurt until well combined. Pour the mixture into a mold or ramekin. Refrigerate for at least 2 hours before serving.

PRESERVES

Place the peaches, sugar, lemon juice, orange juice, and pectin in a small saucepan. Bring the mixture to a simmer and cook for 10 minutes. Cool before serving.

To serve, unmold the Honey Beer Panna Cotta and top with the Peach Preserves and honey or serve in ramekins topped with the preserves and honey.

ACTIVE PREP: 45 minutes
TOTAL TIME: 2 minutes
SERVES: 8–10

1 cup (8 fl oz/237 ml) heavy cream
1 cup sugar
1½ cup mascarpone
1 Tbs (½ fl oz/15 ml) vanilla extract
42–48 ladyfingers
¾ cup (6 fl oz/177 ml) coffee stout, chocolate stout, or porter
½ cup cocoa powder

Fort Collins Brewery Chocolate Stout
(FORT COLLINS, CO)
Goose Island Bourbon County Brand Stout
(CHICAGO, IL)
AleSmith Speedway Stout, or Barrel-Aged
Speedway Stout
(SAN DIEGO, CA)

Beeramisu

In a medium bowl, combine the cream and sugar. With an electric mixer, whip the cream and sugar until firm and fluffy. Add the mascarpone and vanilla and continue whipping for another minute. Chill the mixture for 30 minutes. Place one layer of ladyfingers in the bottom of an 8-inch × 8-inch (20-cm x 20-cm) pan. Brush the ladyfingers liberally with the beer, applying a good soaking. Spread a layer of the mascarpone filling over the ladyfingers. Repeat the layers until the pan is full, making sure that the last layer is the filling. Dust with cocoa powder. Cover and refrigerate for at least 2 hours before serving.

INDEX

INDEX